NB 7131257 9

D0187957

Superbikes
of the seventies

3185211
629.2275

John Nutting

Motor Cycle

Hamlyn
London·New York·Sydney·Toronto

Published by the Hamlyn Publishing Group Limited
London · New York · Sydney · Toronto
Astronaut House, Feltham, Middlesex, England
Copyright © IPC Specialist & Professional Press Limited 1978
Second Impression 1979
All rights reserved. No part of this publication may be reproduced,
stored in a retrieval system, or transmitted, in any form or by any
means, electronic, mechanical, photocopying, recording or otherwise
without the permission of The Hamlyn Publishing Group Limited and
the copyrightholder

ISBN 0600 38222 2

Filmset in Great Britain by Photocomp Limited, Birmingham
Printed in Hong Kong

Contents

Introduction

Superbikes are the pinnacles of manufacturers' development; demonstrations of technological prowess; objects of fantasy and worship; expressions of individuality.

Superbikes have never been so wonderfully diverse as they are today. Whether it is on six-cylinder tarmac rippling sportsters, water-cooled tourers, threes, flat twins, vee-twins or sophisticated fours, the modern motor cyclist can find instant freedom and exhilaration when he rides off on his impressive steed.

Yet it is only a decade since the first real superbike appeared, Honda's CB750 four. Japan showed the way, exploiting the thirst for one-dimensional American travel. Power was – and is – what Americans wanted and that first brilliant effort provided the impetus for others, Britain, Italy, Germany and America, to follow.

The common thread is engine size and power. Ten years ago the best bikes were good for 120 mph; the fastest now can comfortably top 140 mph and rip through the standing quarter-mile in under twelve seconds.

Nevertheless, a second generation of superbikes is appearing. While pleased that such stunning machines existed at all, European motor cyclists regarded first with amusement and later with scorn the poverty of handling associated with the early superbikes; they were fine in a straight line but lamentably wobbly when ridden enthusiastically on twisty continental roads.

The manufacturers recognised this basic shortcoming and achieved new heights of all-round sophistication. Not only do the second generation bikes corner well but maintenance is simplified, with shaft drive and strong engines.

The tenth anniversary of the superbike will be seen too as the year the capacity race started. Kawasaki started with their 1,015 cc Z1R four, Yamaha replied with a 1,101 cc shaft drive dohc four, Laverda opened out their dohc three to 1,115 cc and Honda introduced a 1,047 cc six.

Despite murmurings of discontent from those who regard the superbike as a wasteful indulgence in money and metal, it is here to stay. Factories see it as a necessity to explore the higher levels of performance, if only to show their competitors and buyers alike of their capabilities, for this can reflect on other machines in their ranges.

There is nothing illusory about a superbike. It shamelessly displays engineering design in one of

Three of the most recent additions to the superbike line up:
Right: *from Italy is the 1,115 cc version of the Laverda's twin overhead camshaft three, the 1200.*
Far top: *the fastest and most powerful roadster ever offered for sale, the six-cylinder Honda CBX, which develops 103 bhp at 9,000 rpm for a top speed over 140 mph.*
Far lower: *the shaft drive Yamaha 1100*

the few easily attainable fusions of man and machine.

This book covers twenty of the best superbikes that have appeared in a decade. Outright performance is not the only criteria, and while many of the bikes were good in their day they have been eclipsed by later machines; nevertheless they played a part in the development of the superbike.

Readers will find some machines missing, the latest because they are so new, others because they simply did not become available for a full test. The collection here has been ridden, tested and enjoyed in the course of preparing road test reports for *Motor Cycle*; the texts of these tests have been updated to put each machine into perspective.

I have had the pleasure to ride all the bikes, but I am indebted to Bob Currie and Stewart Boroughs for use of their test material, to Dave Richmond for picture research and Don Morley for the provision of colour photographs.

Bikes that are super have always existed, but the word was coined as recently as 1968. Therefore *Superbikes of the Seventies* is a collection which covers the best of that decade.
JAN

Note: The specifications of the machines covered in this book have differed slightly from market to market.

BMW R100RS

BMW, for so long steeped in a traditionally conservative approach to building motor cycles, have never been regarded as pacesetters. After all the German company has been successfully making bikes since 1923 and the principles that resulted in the latest range of 980 cc models are just the same as they were 55 years ago; that their goals of simplicity, refinement and good handling could be best served by the air-cooled, horizontally-opposed twin with shaft drive.

On the face of it then, the R100RS is a radical departure from the BMW mould. Initially, the striking appearance of the R100RS's streamlined body work hints of a new direction in the Bee-Emm camp. Certainly it is true that few manufacturers have succeeded in selling a fully faired machine. And there is no doubt that the BMW R100RS is a pacesetter. For it raises the state of the 'art' in motor cycle aerodynamic design to a new level. In fact, the R100RS is the logical progression of BMW's basic concept of offering machines which are peerless long-distance cruisers; the fairing merely enables the rider to raise this ability to new levels, levels which are now far

above that offered anywhere else.

Even without the fairing, the biggest of the BMW twins are superlative machines for touring: light, economical and breathlessly relaxed at speed. Exploiting the slim shape to tuck the rider in, BMW have always offered the standard of riding comfort, like the quietness of the exhaust, by which others are judged. The addition of the 'cockpit' merely raises this standard to a new high. With the R100RS, the rider can now enjoy covering massive distances at 100 mph or more and still arrive at his destination fresh. In bad weather he remains dry and clean.

Riding the bike is at first an uncanny experience. The streamlining is so well integrated that the rider never feels aware of it until he glances down at the speedo and realises that he is travelling at 100 mph when he thought he was doing a relaxed 60 mph.

The difference between this and other motor cycle streamling intended for road use is based in the initial BMW concepts. It is not made for increased speed; had this been the aim they would have used a much lower profile. What they wanted was to insulate the rider from wind pressure while using the normal riding stance, and use the fairing to provide a degree of aerodynamic downthrust to improve the stability at high speeds, the lack of which was becoming embarrasing on the R100S version of the 980 cc twin with its small handlebar screen.

Using the Pinifarina wind tunnel in Italy BMW achieved just those aims.

To all intents and purposes BMW have created a bike that behaves just like any other solo – but has none of the problems that make a mockery of the performance claims of the competitors. Although many other bikes can easily better 125 mph, in real practical terms this is virtually impossible because of high handlebars and awkward footrests.

With the claimed power output of the R100RS engine, 70 bhp at 7,250 rpm, in mind, our top speed figures may be considerably lower than expected. The mean two-way top speed of 113·8 mph obtained at MIRA is slower than many seven-fifties, and the standing quarter mile time of 14·2 seconds is lower than the unfaired R100/7 BMW. But it has to be remembered that these figures were taken with the rider sitting upright, and then the true picture comes to light – on most other unstreamlined bikes this would be almost impossible! And that top speed can be maintained without tiring the rider as long as there is fuel in the tank.

The other advantages of the fairing are immediately apparent whether you ride the R100RS slow or fast. In town at relatively modest speeds the screen still protects the rider from the weather as well as offering a bright object for other road users to see. And the handling is perceptibly more stable at speeds over 50 mph. BMW claim that the wedge shape of the screen and the spoiler either side give 17 per cent extra downthrust compared to the naked machine.

BMW also claim a six per cent cut in drag. While this shows as a bonus in top speed if the rider remains sitting upright (if he crouched down on the naked bike he would go faster still), the main advantage is one of improved fuel economy.

Cruising at a steady 100 mph, the R100RS returned 42 mpg, which combined with the capacity of the $5\frac{1}{4}$ gallon tank offers the rider a range of at least 200 miles. Most other bikes at this speed would be struggling to better 30–35 mpg with ranges of half the Bee-Emm's.

At a more casual (and legal in the UK) 70 mph, the benefits are even more startling. At this speed the bike returned 57·6 mpg! But the most was made of the RS's long leggedness and our overall test consumption over 1,300 miles was 44·2 mpg including the MIRA tests and some commuting.

The only drawback of the addition of the fairing is its weight. With it the R100RS weighs in at over 500 lb (although this is still less than most smaller seven fifties) and the flat out acceleration takes a dive.

The R100RS engine, unlike its Japanese competition, is remarkably unsophisticated. A simple pushrod opposed twin with very oversquare dimensions (94 × 70·6 mm), it is lower, flexible and light. And with a massive flywheel very sweet in use. Only mechanical noise is the tapping of the valve rockers.

Specification

Engine: 980 cc (94 × 70·6 mm) overhead valve, horizontally-opposed flat-twin. Light-alloy cylinder head and barrels; cast-iron liners. Two plain main bearings; plain big ends. Wet sump lubrication with Eaton-type pump and replaceable paper oil filter. Compression ratio, 9·5 to 1. Two 40-mm choke Bing constant-velocity carburettors with cable-operated cold-start jets; paper element air filter. Claimed maximum power, 70 bhp at 7,250 rpm. Maximum torque, 55·7 lb-ft at 5,500 rpm.

Transmission: Crankshaft-mounted single-plate dry clutch. Helical gears to five-speed gearbox. Overall ratios: 13·2, 8·58, 6·27, 5·01 and 4·5 to 1. Shaft final drive (ratio, 3 to 1 with optional 2·91 to 1).

Electrical Equipment: Coil ignition. 12-volt, 28-amp-hour battery and 240-watt field-excited alternator. 7·5-in diameter headlamp with 60/55-watt quartz-halogen main bulb. Five fuses in headlamp.

Brakes: Cable and hydraulically-operated 10·25-in diameter twin perforated disc front, 7·87-in drum rear.

Tyres: Metzeler, 3·25 × H19-in ribbed front, 4·00 × H18-in patterned rear. Light-alloy rims.

Suspension: Telescopic front fork with adjustable steering damper. Pivoted rear fork with three-position manual multirate spring preload adjustment.

Frame: Welded duplex cradle with oval spine and bolted-on rear subframe.

Dimensions: Wheelbase, 58·5 in; seat height, 32·5 in; ground clearance, 6·5 in; overall width, 29·5 in; trail 3·5 in; turning circle, 17 ft 10 in; all unladen.

Weight: 511 lb including approximately one gallon of fuel.

Fuel Capacity: 5·25 UK gal (6·3 US gal) including 7 pt reserve.

Sump Oil Capacity: 4 pt.

Manufacturer: Bayerische Motoren Werke AG, D-8000 Munchen 80, West Germany.

Performance

Maximum Speeds (Mean): 113·8 mph; 111·4 mph with rider in oversuit sitting normally.

Best One-way Speed: 115·9 mph – dry track, slight tail wind.

Braking Distance – from 30 mph: 27 ft 6 in.

Fuel Consumption: 44·2 miles/UK gal (36·7 miles/US gal).

Oil Consumption: negligible.

Minimum Non-snatch Speed: 14 mph in top gear.

Speedo Accuracy:

Indicated mph	30	40	50	60	70	80	90
Actual mph	27·4	36·6	45·8	55·3	64·8	75·5	86·1

The main attraction, however, of the R100RS engine is its flexibility, even though it is the most highly tuned of the three 980 cc flat twins in the BMW range. It is this flexibility which makes the bike one of the most formidable on the road.

Once into top gear on the five-speed gearbox, there was rarely any need to change down unless coming to a stop, even in town. Solid torque is delivered from 2,000 rpm, and although this power unit is not one of the smoothest the bike leaps forward with the slightest throttle opening.

Mid-range pick-up is where the R100RS scores best and this is demonstrated most impressively in top gear acceleration from 50 mph.

Compared to say, the super sports Honda CB750F, which over the standing quarter is over a second quicker, the R100RS accelerates like a rocket from 50 mph in top, and although the Honda catches up slightly as it hits its power band it fails to make up the initial loss.

Nevertheless the R100RS is not perfection from stem to stern, for of its high-speed touring role, where it is incomparable, it can be uncomfortable.

To allow the fairing to be narrower, the handlebar is shorter and slightly lower than on the other BMWs; this throws more weight onto the rider's wrists, and it can be tiring when the bike is ridden in town for any length of time.

There are also a couple of annoying vibration periods which, although they do not detract from the high level of comfort, annoy because they stand out against the general standard of sophistication.

First, torque pulse vibration occurs when opening up at low revs, and can only be minimised by very careful synchronisation of the carburettors. There is also a period of resonance between 80 and 85 mph which renders the mirrors useless. Fortunately, the clarity of the mirror images is restored at 100 mph.

The gearchange in the three higher ratios is silent and slick, but equally noiseless changes in the lower gears still call for a co-ordination of controls, particularly in the stop-go of city traffic.

Otherwise the response to the controls is impeccable. The black hand levers, by Magura, are well contoured for comfort and the clutch is light and smooth with a wide contact point. The throttle has considerably less movement than on earlier BMWs, yet retains a light action. The Hella switchgear is improved, with longer thumb switches for the dip and indicator.

BMW roadholding and handling has always been very good and the steering is top notch, thanks to the forward-mounted axle contributing to low inertia around the steering axis, an aspect improved further by moving the headlight into the fairing.

Even with a fractionally larger turning circle, the R100RS can still be turned feet up in the average road width.

Changes have been made to the suspension: some good, some bad. The long, soft action is retained, although the front fork has slightly stronger springs than the R100S to counteract the downward thrust created by the stream-lining. The rear units have multi-rate springs for optimum ride comfort with a variety of loads.

In fast going over bumpy roads, the bike handles superbly with an uncanny combination of ride quality and directional stability. In the wet, the Metzeler tyres give safe and predictable grip without a sudden breakaway.

However, when ridden more sedately, the R100RS shows the other side of the coin. Excessive seal friction and heavy compression damping in the front forks virtually lock up the front suspension over short sharp bumps like pot holes and manhole covers. In a short ride in town, the RS reveals none of the luxury qualities that you would expect of it. It is very much a bike that has to be ridden hard and fast to appreciate its best qualities. Although attractive and impressively styled to match the fairing the one plus a half RS seat is of little use in day to day riding, being too short to accommodate any but the smallest of passengers; the S seat offered on the 1978 models as standard is more sensible. Under the lockable seat are a bin for bits and pieces plus the toolkit trough and, in the nose of the seat padding, a first aid kit. A rubber-covered security chain is hidden up inside the main frame tube.

Finished in dusted silver with blue lining with gold as an option, the R100RS has superb paintwork.

Quality of construction shows a singularly uncompromising attitude to design that is typified by the use of tapered and oval tubing for the frame, exceptionally powerful and reliable electrics with a searing halogen headlamp and a massive 28-amp-hour battery, plus a pair of stunning Fiamm air horns. The electric starting is as reliable as ever. Appreciation of the need for easy maintenance is shown by the quickly detachable wheels and a centre stand that is at the balance point of the bike.

The brakes and wheels too are of the highest quality. For 1978, the rear drum brake was replaced with a perforated disc similar to the pair fitted to the front wheel. All three discs are extremely progressive in action and work better than most in the rain. Wheels are now the Italian made cast-alloy units originally shown on the 1977 prototypes.

Such are the details that push the price well above the norm but contribute to a refined and practical machine.

With Honda, Moto Guzzi and Yamaha offering shaft-drive 1,000 cc touring machines with dazzling performance figures there is plenty of choice for the mega-buck touring rider. But only BMW still offer a machine that is really different and practical for high speed use as well as having that touch of quite exclusivity.

Few things compare with the thrill of charging comfortably and unobtrusively through the night behind the cosy glow of the instruments in the cockpit, the time on the quartz clock seeming to slow down with the way the R100RS can compress the miles.

Cockpit view of the R100RS shows the instrumentation; speedo and rev counter plus a voltmeter and quartz clock in the top of the fairing
Far left: accessibility to the flat twin engine is not hampered by the fairing

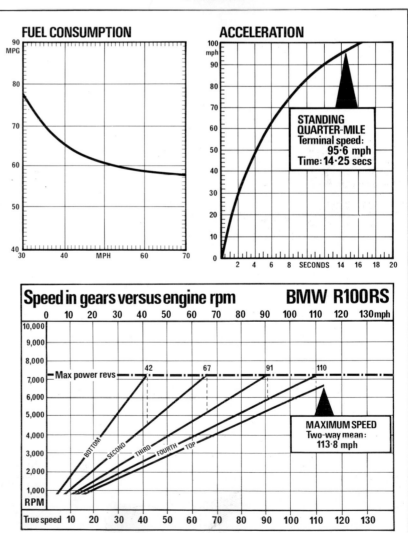

FUEL CONSUMPTION

ACCELERATION

STANDING QUARTER-MILE
Terminal speed: 95·6 mph
Time: 14·25 secs

Speed in gears versus engine rpm   BMW R100RS

Max power revs

MAXIMUM SPEED
Two-way mean: 113·8 mph

Ducati 860 GTS

As far as their objectives of fine handling and usable road performance are concerned, Ducati have always had their priorities right. Few manufacturers have been able to equal the combination of flexibility and smoothness offered by Ducati's vee-twin engines. Their record in such demanding races as the Barcelona 24-hours at the round-the-houses Montjuich Park is testimony enough to the quality of the Ducati's steering and roadholding.

Lamentably, however, poor detail finishing and electrical equipment has given Ducati a reputation for rough quality that will take a long time to wear off.

The Ducati 860 GTS, introduced in 1976, was the first indication that the factory was able to offer a machine finished to the same level as the Japanese. It was based on the Guigiaro-styled 860 GT that had proved to be so impractical on the road. The GTS was offered with a more sensible seat and tank and makes a much more agreeable tourer.

Like all the big Ducatis, the 860 GTS has the vee-twin engine so loved by purists of motor cycle design. Being a 90-degree engine, it offers a pleasant lack of vibration and a slim profile that allows the unit to be slung low in the frame for a low centre of gravity.

The frame itself is sensibly made of straight tubing and incorporates the engine as a part of the structure. Triangulated and very strong, it offers tremendous rigidity from the use of thick-walled tubes – a feature that, while it may add a few pounds to the overall weight of the machine, more than offsets this with Ducati's almost legendary high speed handling.

Drawbacks of the Ducati approach to its engine design are that the complexity of the bevel and shaft drive to the overhead camshafts make it notoriously expensive to machine and assemble. Fans of the distinctive mechanical melodies made by such a layout will however be pleased to know that the costs of redesigning the valve gear with quieter toothed belts, as on the more recent 500 cc vee-twin, are far greater in the long run than the current production costs and we shall be able to have the pleasure of riding the 860 vee-twin Ducatis for some time yet.

Another drawback of the Ducati approach to the vee-twin is that its length limits the minimum length of the machine. With a wheelbase of exactly 5 ft, the Ducati 860 GTS is one of the longest machines of its type. While conferring a degree of stability during cornering rarely experienced on other machines, such a feature detracts from the bike's manoeuvrability at low speeds and requires a greater angle of lean for a given cornering speed. This means that any clearance advantage offered by the narrow width of the engine unit is more quickly eaten up. As a result, the frame and suspension limits are rarely approached.

Ducati have persevered through the eight years since the first 750 cc models were introduced. In 1974, the 864 cc version with a bore and stroke of 86 by 74·4 mm was introduced with newer styling for the crankcases and the option for an electric starter.

Demand for a more practical big bore Ducati as an alternative to the Super Sports desmodromic production racer led to the 860 GTS and the more recent 900 Darmah, which has the desmo valve gear of the sportster but with a softer state of tune and more up-to-date styling with Japanese instrumentation and cast magnesium wheels.

The 860 GTS is nevertheless a good balance between specification and price, being offered at some £500 less than the Darmah. The most obvious difference between the GTS and its predecessors is the fat fuel tank with a 4 gallon capacity. There is also the low and wide seat. Instrumentation was taken from the obsolete 750 Sport with the British Smiths' clocks mounted on an alloy plate with the ignition lock between them.

The electronic ignition fitted to the first eight-sixties meant that the kick starter had to be given a hefty swing to fire up the bike, a very awkward task with the kick starter so close to the footrests. But the electric starter, which is mounted atop the primary gearcase with the relay under the nearside side cover and connected by a rod to the engaging gears, makes starting easy. It is just a matter of lifting the mixture enrichening lever and punching the little button on the left handlebar console.

Once running, everything that made the old sports singles like Velocettes so appealing – a classical and unique blend of mechanical sound and a broad road flexibility – is recalled on the Ducati. Its road performance is superb. While not immensely powerful compared to many 900 cc or 1,000 cc bikes, tractability and low-end punch of the Ducati makes the bike a daunting competitor on twisty and demanding roads. Snapping open the throttles of the 32-mm choke Delorto carburettors is rewarded by an instant kick in the back and this happens whether riding through town or whistling along the open road. The top speed of 103 mph with the rider sitting upright is comparable to many bigger machines.

Although the bike has an excellent five-speed gearbox, with a very pleasant change mechanism, there is very little reason to use it. Once into top gear there is hardly a circumstance which requires changing down. Even baulking by slower traffic at motorway speeds is seldom frustrating, as with a twist of the right hand the big vee-twin surges forward with hardly a hiccup.

Like many similar flexible bikes, the performance is never shown up to apparent advantage in the absolute performance figures. The addition of improved intake silencing and exhaust pipes which emit a deep drone has chopped the top end torque to the degree that there is no reason to rev

the unit beyond 6,500 rpm, although Ducati quote the maximum power of around 60 bhp at 7,000 rpm. The weight has crept up too. At 520 lb the 860 GTS is the heaviest ever from the Bologna factory. This shows in the slower quarter mile time of 13·85 sec, with a terminal speed of 97 mph.

The test bike had also had its overall gearing lowered by an extra tooth on the rear wheel sprocket. This gave a top gear ratio of 5·04 to 1 and while improving the mid-range response at around 70 mph it lowered the bottom gear ratios to a level that made it difficult to prevent near-uncontrollable wheelspin during standing starts, which lost additional time.

For the state of tune of the Ducati, it meant that it was revving at an unusually high 4,700 rpm at 70 mph. Flat out in top gear with the rider flat on the tank at a mean 114·9 mph the engine was revving well over its power peak, at 7,700 rpm. It is possible that Ducati geared the machine with a normally seated rider in mind, but it is also certain that the bike would have been much faster through the timing lights with higher gearing and would probably have been quicker through the quarter mile.

On the positive side though was the sheer pulling power of the GTS. Hills would be flattened with hardly any throttle movement, while at the test strip, it accelerated from 40 mph to 92·5 mph in top gear in a quarter mile, the best figure for that test ever recorded for any bike.

Ninety-degree vee-twins are appealing for their perfect primary balance. In practice, however, the bigger the engine gets, the bigger are the secondary forces; in the case of the Ducati these act at approximately 35 degrees from the horizontal and at twice the frequency of the engine revs. At high speed this is shown by a buzz through the handlebar and footrests, but it only became bothersome at around 5,000 rpm.

Fuel consumption was improved compared with the GT version, by about 3 mpg; this was possibly due to the slightly higher compression ratio of 9·8 to 1. Using four-star fuel, the GTS returned 43·1 mpg overall, dropping to 38 mpg at the test strip while up to 47 mpg was possible with careful riding. Oil consumption was minimal – just as well, as the filler plug at the front of the sump is the worst encountered for undoing and topping up.

Ducati are one of the few manufacturers who offer footrests with height adjustment. Set properly they give the Duke a comfortable riding position to 85 mph although the new, lower dual seat lacks padding enough for a comfortable ride over 100 miles. For a vee-twin the Ducati footrests are surprisingly wide at 27 inches tip to tip, and this produces a cornering clearance problem.

The very strong frame and taut steering of the GTS encourages brisk bend swinging and the footrests can be worn down very easily without riding hard. The footrests can be raised easily but this produces an awkward riding position.

This is despite very stiff suspension. Short travel Ceriani front forks are used, but these are not comparable in quality to some Cerianis we have experienced. Chattery over ripples, they lacked the lithe feel normally associated with Italian suspension.

To lessen the effects of the long wheelbase, radical steering geometry with a 60½ degree head angle and a massive 5 inches of trail are used. The effect is to make the steering extremely taut at speed but heavy around town. Plenty of physical force is needed to swing the bike through sharp bends and a degree of precision that leaves little room for mistakes when riding fast.

Fortunately the big Metzeler tyres were very grippy in the dry, in strong contrast to their

---

Specification

Engine: 864 cc (86 × 74·4 mm) overhead camshaft, 90° vee-twin. Light-alloy barrel and heads; cast-iron liners. Three ball main bearings; needle-roller big ends. Wet sump lubrication; gear pump. Compression ratio, 9·8 to 1. Two 32-mm choke Delorto carburettors with accelerator pumps and cable-operated cold-start jets; paper element air filters. Claimed maximum power, 67·7 bhp at 7,000 rpm. Maximum torque, 61 lb-ft at 4,000 rpm.

Transmission: Primary helical gears (ratio, 2·187 to 1). Wet, multiplate clutch and five-speed gearbox. Overall ratios: 12·7, 8·88, 6·84, 5·68 and 5·04 to 1. Final drive by 0·625 × 0·375-in chain (ratio, 39/15). Mph at 1,000 rpm in top gear, 14·9.

Electrical Equipment: Electronic ignition. 12-volt, 32-amp-hour battery, 200-watt alternator and voltage regulator. 7-in diameter Aprilia headlamp with 60/55-watt quartz halogen main bulb. Four fuses.

Brakes: Brembo 11-in diameter double disc front with double-acting calipers, 7·875-in diameter drum rear, cable operated.

Tyres: Metzeler, 3·50 × H18-in block C66 front, 120/90 × H18-in block C88 rear.

Suspension: Ceriani telescopic front fork. Pivoted rear fork with Marzocchi dampers with five-position spring preload.

Frame: Welded duplex tube type incorporating engine unit.

Dimensions: Wheelbase, 60·25 in; ground clearance, 7 in; seat height, 31·25 in; handlebar width, 28 in; castor angle, 60·5°; trail, 4·9 in; turning circle, 15 ft 2 in; all unladen.

Weight: 520 lb including one gallon of fuel.

Fuel Capacity: 4·1 UK gal (4·9 US gal) including 2 pt reserve.

Sump Oil Capacity: 6·5 pt.

Manufacturer: Ducati Meccanica SpA, Via A. C. Ducati, 3, Cas. Postale 313, 40100 Bologna.

Performance

Maximum Speeds (Mean): 114·9 mph; 102·8 mph with rider in two-piece outfit sitting normally.

Best One-way Speed: 118·7 mph – dry track, 5 mph three-quarter tail wind.

Braking Distance – from 30 mph: 30 ft 10 in.

Fuel Consumption: 43·1 miles/UK gal (35·8 miles/US gal).

Oil Consumption: Negligible.

Minimum Non-snatch Speed: 24 mph in top gear.

Speedo Accuracy:

Indicated kmh	50	75	100	125
Actual kmh	46·3	71·2	99·1	127·4

British instruments are used on the Ducati 860 GTS with below the dials a row of light-emitting diode warning lights
Far right: drawback of the Ducati vee-twin layout is the arranging of the air filters. Above the swinging arm pivot is the relay for the starter and its connecting linkage

apparently poor wet grip; a problem that was tracked down to misaligned wheels. On most other bikes this can be corrected at the rear-wheel chain adjusters, but the Ducati has eccentric adjusters at the swinging arm mount which preclude anything but frame straightening.

Double discs are now offered on the GTS front wheel and the power provided is phenomenal. In fact these brakes were so powerful that the 30 mph stopping distance tests revolved around a trick to prevent the front wheel locking.

The rear drum was merely average by comparison. It faded in normal use and was insensitive in an emergency.

The Ducati's electrics are a vast improvement on previous models. The transistorised ignition is maintenance free and the voltage control unit for the massive 32-amp-hour battery is electronic too. The 60-watt quartz-halogen headlamp sends out a strong, safe beam that is ideal for quick night riding. Only the awkward hand switches and the microscopic light-emitting diode warning lamps spoil the electrics.

The tools, which sit in a plastic tray under the lockable seat are adequate for most of the tasks required, but the spanners were brittle and broke if used clumsily.

Faults were confined to a speedo that failed towards the end of the 700 mile test and some corrosion on the main fuse that blacked out the bike. There was no prop stand but the main stand was easy to use.

The Ducati 860 GTS has such a pleasing character that grows on you that owners find it easy to ignore the poor chrome and soft paint just for that thundering silky urge of the big vee-twin with the cantering exhaust note.

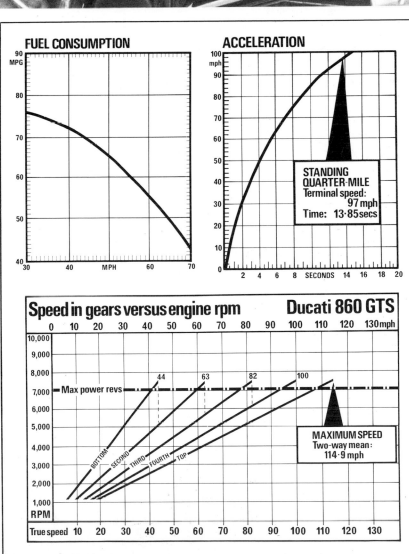

FUEL CONSUMPTION

ACCELERATION

STANDING QUARTER-MILE
Terminal speed: 97 mph
Time: 13·85 secs

Speed in gears versus engine rpm   **Ducati 860 GTS**

Max power revs

44   63   82   100

BOTTOM   SECOND   THIRD   FOURTH   TOP

MAXIMUM SPEED
Two-way mean: 114·9 mph

Harley-Davidson FXE-1200

There is nothing quite like gunning down the highway at 70 mph on a big Harley-Davidson vee-twin. Perhaps it is the overwhelming presence of the vast engine churing around at a lazy 3,250 rpm or perhaps it is the rangy, built-like-a-truck feel that is so appealing. Either way, there is something instantly attractive about a motor cycle that almost seems alive.

It rumbles, it cranks, it clatters and it vibrates – but what motor cycle retaining any connection with the grass roots of two-wheel travel didn't? Or so the Harley buff's argument goes. Therein lies the reason *why* there is nothing quite like a Harley – other makers have seen fit to bring wider appeal to their bikes by modern design and refinement. Meanwhile Harley-Davidson remain staunchly in the traditionalist's camp with their 20-year-old design in the biggest of their vee-twins, the FXE-1200.

All the same, riding a Harley-Davidson is a unique experience. For a start, you do not so much ride the bike but sit in it, the saddle being somewhere at axle height and the controls somewhere about 3 ft above it. And no sooner have you sunk into that deep saddle than you start scowling and snarling at your fellow road users. The Harley is that *bad*, and the other guys had better know it.

Fantasies, however, last only so long, and all the imagery in the world cannot cover up the fact that the Harley is rough and, in the case of the FXE1200, over-priced when looked at realistically.

The twelve-hundred engine is the bigger of the two Harley-Davidson 45 degree vee-twins and famous for powering the romantic FLH1200 Electra-Glide tourer. The Super Glide is the cut-and-shut version, a lighter (if 585 lb with a gallon of fuel can be called light), leaner and more esoteric machine with its western droop 'bars, 2½-gallon tank, banana seat and abbreviated fenders. There is one concession to civility, signified

by the E suffix in the FXE-1200 model number, and that is the electric starter, a necessity if you prefer riding to sweating up a lather by the side of the road. But even the starter motor is in character. Switching on with the ignition lock hidden between the cylinders and applying just a small amount of choke, the mechanism grinds into action and the motor bursts into life with a rumplety-rumplety exhaust note which, thanks to the latest style exhaust system, is muted very effectively.

The rest of the machine is still pure vintage, however. The result is that the exhaust system severely reduces the performance as well.

Harley-Davidson claim a maximum power output of around 65 bhp at a leisurely 5,500 rpm, but the actual power fell far short of this in test and the best we could extract out of the bike at MIRA was a two-way mean speed of 108 mph, and a best run of almost 114 mph. Flat-out acceleration, too, is hardly in the superbike class with a standing quarter-mile time of 15·3 seconds. Not that this matters too much on the road. For the redeeming feature of the FXE is torque – mountains of it. Right from the outset the modestly tuned 1,207 cc engine makes it obvious that it does not need to be rushed to provide the goods. With the peculiar Bendix carburettor (now replaced by a Japanese Keihin equivalent), which acts more like an on-off switch at small openings, the reaction to a tweak of the grip from low revs is instantaneous and monumental.

As a rule, 2,500 rpm was more than enough to maintain a clear road ahead through the four-speed gearbox and even for modest cruising, as these revs corresponded to over 50 mph in top gear.

This was just as well, since vibrations start in earnest at 3,200 rpm, buzzing the instruments frantically, and only marginally smoothing out towards the rev limit at 6,000 rpm. The happiest cruising speed was at 3,500 rpm, where the chugging motor had plenty in hand for instant overtaking.

Despite the laid-back feel of the bike, its crudity cannot be overlooked. In addition to the rough carburation and painful vibration, the transmission is poor, with only a tough damper on the crankshaft to take up the shocks, and the suspension is hard. You ride the Harley in a series of bangs and clanks. The non-unit gearbox has a linkage-operated one-down, three-up lever, and while much better than the box on the Sportster XL-1000 it still shows its age. Neutral is easy to find, but the unit is clonky, most gears dropping into place with the caress of a pile-driver.

In contrast, the dry clutch in a massive alloy casting is perfect. Light in action, the take-up is so smooth that slipping it at low speed to cover up the snatching transmission is easy.

By reputation, Harley handling is pretty foul, but we found the steering very good on the FXE. The low engine and riding position makes the bike very easy to flick through bends, although the lack of ground clearance, even with the rear suspension units jacked up to the highest pre-load, leads to a grinding side stand and footrests in corners.

Longer than the Sportster, the riding position takes some getting used to, but with the deeply-padded seat is comfortable, the only real criticism being the way the hands tend to slip off the downward-angled and smooth grips.

The hard suspension, weak frame and slippery tyres lead to the main handling faults on the FXE-1200. Both front and rear spring travel is

short and the lack of rigidity in the frame can cause the bike to get out of shape easily. Bumpy corners mean plenty of action for the rider. In the wet the Goodyear tyres indicate forcefully that they were never intended for greasy roads. Pulling away from stops in the rain is a balancing act between traction of the big 5·10 × 16-in rear tyre and throttle opening.

Although disc brakes are used at the front and rear, they continue the theme of crudity. Both brakes are powerful enough to lock the wheels,

Specification

Engine: 1,207 cc (87·3 × 100·8 mm) overhead valve, 45° vee-twin. Light-alloy cylinder heads and cast-iron barrels. One double-roller, one single-roller main bearing with outrigger bush on timing side. Dry sump lubrication; gear pump. Compression ratio, 8 to 1. One 38-mm choke Bendix carburettor with accelerator pump and plunger-operated choke; foam-mesh air filter. Claimed maximum power, 65 bhp at 5,500 rpm.

Transmission: Duplex 0·5 × 0·31 in primary chain. Dry, multiplate clutch and non-unit four-speed gearbox with direct top gear. Overall ratios: 10·25, 6·24, 4·21 and 3·42 to 1. Final drive chain, 0·625 × 0·375 in. Mph at 1,000 rpm in top gear, 22.

Electrical Equipment: Coil ignition with single contact breaker, 12-volt, 18-amp-hour battery, 300-watt alternator with electronic voltage control. 5·5-in diameter headlamp with approximately 55-watt sealed-beam unit. Starter motor; thermal circuit breakers.

Brakes: Hydraulically operated 11·75-in diameter chromed-steel disc front, 9·75-in diameter disc rear. Floating calipers.

Tyres: Goodyear MM90 3·50 × 19-in. ribbed front, MT90 5·10 × 16-in rear studded.

Suspension: Telescopic front fork, 3·5 in travel. Pivoted rear fork with three-position spring preload adjustment.

Frame: Duplex loop cradle with cast lugs.

Dimensions: Wheelbase, 61·75 in; ground clearance, 6 in; seat height, 29 in; footrest height, 11 in; handlebar width, 29 in; turning circle, 14 ft 6 in.

Weight: 585 lb including one gallon of fuel.

Fuel Capacity: 2·75 UK gal (3·3 US gal) including 6 pt reserve.

Sump Oil Capacity: 7 pt.

Manufacturer: Harley-Davidson Motorcycles, 3700 West Juneau, Milwaukee, Wisconsin 53201.

Performance

Maximum Speeds (Mean): 108·3 mph; 100·4 mph with rider seated normally in oversuit.

Best One-way Speed: 113·8 mph – dry track, slight tail wind.

Braking Distance – from 30 mph: 30 ft 3 in.

Fuel Consumption: 38·1 miles/UK gal (31·6 miles/US gal).

Oil Consumption: 700 mpp.

Minimum Non-snatch Speed: 18 mph in top gear.

Speedo Accuracy:

Indicated kmh	50	60	70	80	90	100	110	120
Actual kmh	43·6	53·1	62·5	72·6	83·4	94·2	104·2	114·2

but the calipers rattle badly, the rear unit tending to grab as well. The controls do not help. Like the clutch, the reach on the front-brake hand lever is excessive and the rider needs to lift his foot off the rest to reach the rear brake.

Fed by a massive alternator mounted behind the primary drive on the crankshaft, the electrical system is modern enough but suffered from silly faults. The size of the headlamp (5½ in), belies the power of the sealed unit which throws a healthy spot main and wide dipped beam. But the battery capacity is too low and plenty of night use meant that the engine failed to spin over on the button next morning. Also, chafed ignition wires which shorted out demonstrated the use of the thermal contact breakers, which reconnect the supply when the fault is corrected.

The indicators are operated by press buttons

on either handgrip, a very unsatisfactory method when you have to manipulate the other controls at the same time. On the good side, the stentorian horn is fabulous. You not only hear it but feel it too, it's so powerful.

Only a prop stand is fitted, but it does have a locking mechanism to prevent the machine rolling away on a slope.

In general use, the FXE-1200 Harley does not show up as well as the Sportster. Fuel consumption never varied much from the 40 mpg and, indicating a poor setting-up of the carburettor, the steady speed fuel consumption readings hardly varied between 30 mph to 70 mph.

Oil leaks from the chaincase and the pushrod tubes contributed mainly to the heavy oil consumption of 700 miles to the pint. In practice, the oil tank is replenished from the small dipstick hole on the side as the seat needs to be unscrewed for access to the main cap, and no tools are supplied.

This does not sound very promising, but the reasons why someone should spend over £2,000 on such a machine are varied anyway. Perhaps the magic moment when you charge out of a 50 mph bend, change into top at 2,500 revs, and chug off into the horizon in a dream is one of them!

Rider's view of the handlebar shows the big rubber mounted grips and button-operated direction indicators Below: there is no mistaking the 1,207 cc 45 degree vee-twin. Inside the big transmission cover is a dry clutch driving a four-speed gearbox

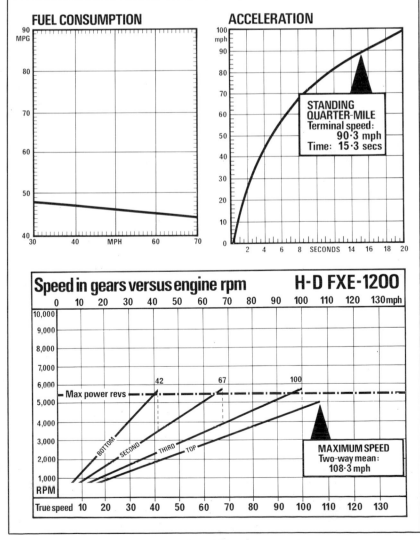

FUEL CONSUMPTION

ACCELERATION

STANDING QUARTER-MILE
Terminal speed: 90·3 mph
Time: 15·3 secs

Speed in gears versus engine rpm **H-D FXE-1200**

Max power revs

42   67   100

BOTTOM   SECOND   THIRD   TOP

MAXIMUM SPEED
Two-way mean: 108·3 mph

True speed 10 20 30 40 50 60 70 80 90 100 110 120 130

Harley-Davidson XLCR-1000

Black power hit the roads of America when Harley-Davidson's cafe racer XLCR-1000, originally shown as a styling exercise in 1974, was put into production three years later. It was a radical departure from the Harleys that built a legend, but it was every bit as exciting as its menacing midnight looks promised. Claimed by the Milwaukee factory to be the fastest road-going bike they had ever produced, the XLCR is a bike in the European mould, nimble as a cat and slim as a dart. Yet underneath it is pure Harley. Wind on the fat twistgrip and the 61 cubic inch vee-twin motor rumbles you forward with all the latent power of a steam locomotive.

Can the XLCR catch on in America, its home?

If the Florida scene around Daytona 200 time is any reflection of the Stateside trends then, after their brief excursion into the limelight in the mid-1970s, cafe racers with their rear-set footrests and back-breaking racing crouch riders are as much a minority interest as ever.

There are hordes of choppers. And touring bikes are almost universal, decked out in an identical manner with Vetter touring fairings enclosing the tape deck and CB radios and enough luggage gear to dwarf a Cadillac. American mainstream motor cycling means covering hundreds of miles on ruler straight highways or cruising down to the shopping mall for a couple of six packs. Neither encourage the

use of tricked-out racing equipment.

But in Europe the XLCR is a complete change from the normal Harleys – which are low, bulky and agricultural. It has a new appeal to the rider who spends more time on – and revels in – twisty roads.

Although it has plenty in common with the chopper-style Harleys, the XLCR feels like a sportster should feel – responsive and nimble, and the antithesis of an Electra-Glide.

It was originally designed by Harley's Director of Styling, William G. Davidson, brother of the President, John A. Davidson. He based it on the front half of a 1,000 cc Sportster engine and frame and mounted on the rear the back end of the XR750 dirt track racer with its longer swinging arm and more vertical suspension units. A small black tank and solo racing seat almost straight off the racer, complemented by a BMW-style top half fairing on the handlebar, completed the bodywork.

The cycle parts were given all the looks of modern racing tackle. Wheels are seven-spoke light-alloy castings by Morris. Brakes are double discs on the front wheel and a single on the rear, all operated by floating calipers. Tyres are the latest sports covers by Goodyear, in wide 3·75 and 4·25 profiles on 19-in front and 18-in rims respectively.

Chugging through Daytona Beach the XLCR felt decidedly alien, much more like a European machine than the usual Harley-Davidsons that we have become used to. The racing style riding position is remarkably comfortable. You lean forward over the sculptured tank and grip a straight handlebar. The seat with its press-studded cover is deep enough to keep the aches away. And the footrests are mounted so that the weight is placed evenly on all the contact points.

The controls are pure Harley though. The grips are fat and smooth and the hand levers, while very effective and handy, look like hand carved alloy. Switchgear, too, is bulky and crude and retains the novel but awkward press buttons on each console for the direction indicators.

As on the 1977 bikes, the gearchange is on the 'Japanese' left side with a reverse lever, while the rear-brake lever is a massive forging of unbreakable proportions that looks as if it was liberated from a truck chassis; it operates the rear disc through a Kelsey Hayes master cylinder.

For boulevarde cruising the XLCR is pleasant enough. At moderate speeds the steering has a light and neutral feel that makes the bike a natural bend swinger. And with such massive punch at low revs the engine encourages a relaxed approach without using the gearbox. But if you attack your riding with more verve, the bike takes on a different character as it is pushed harder through bumpy or fast bends.

The suspension is by the Japanese Kayaba factory and compares both in appearance and performance with the sort of equipment found on Japanese bikes of the early 1970s, in other words, not very impressive.

The XLCR is stiffly sprung as well as offering a

Despite the different lengths of the pipes, Harley-Davidson have used this novel exhaust system on the XLCR sportster
Far right: it may be a cafe racer but the XLCR's handlebar layout is pure Harley with chunky grips and controls

large degree of resistance to the absorption of tarmac seams and joins, both of which spoil the comfort and the handling. The flimsy rear fork does not contribute greatly to the overall stability, as the bike bounces along the road with the usual Harley oblivion to the more sophisticated needs of today's motor cyclist. The vibration, too, becomes more than normal

mortals can usually bear over more than half an hour of riding.

Like all Harley-Davidsons, the focal point of the XLCR is its massive vee-twin engine. Unchanged in general specification from the XLCH Sportster, the 45-degree twin has a charm all of its own, which is more than a little influenced by the vintage appearance of the cast-iron cylinders and heads. Bore and stroke are very under-square, in contrast to current trends, with dimensions of 81 by 96·8 mm for an overall swept volume of 997 cc. In Harley tradition, the cylinders are mounted on crankcases that contain crank flywheels of monstrous dimensions and the connecting-rod big ends are not side-by-side, but have a split rear big end that encases the front one. The big overhead valves are pushrod operated with the carburettor between the cylinders.

Concessions to modern practice are unit construction and electric starting; in fact the one-time ritual of firing up the beast is removed entirely as there is no kick starter. What electrical components there are prove to be as massive as ever, with a solid looking dynamo nestling between the front cylinder and splayed frame tubes and a bulky battery over the clutch housing. Special for the XLCR are hand-finished and carefully assembled power units. These are tested for power and the more potent examples are sidelined for use in the XLCR series, the rest going back to the Sportster line.

Harley-Davidson claim a maximum power of 61 to 62 bhp at 6,200 rpm for the standard engines so this is more than likely to be exceeded by the XLCR units. Whatever it is, Harley-Davidson give the bike a 12-month and 12,000

Specification
Engine: 997·5 cc (81 × 96·8 mm) overhead valve, 45° vee-twin. Cast-iron heads and barrels. Dry sump lubrication. Compression ratio, 9 to 1. Keihin 38-mm choke carburettor with accelerator pump; paper element air filter. Claimed maximum power, 61 bhp at 6,200 rpm. Maximum torque, 52 lb-ft at 3,800 rpm.
Transmission: Primary triplex chain. Wet, multiplate clutch and four-speed gearbox. Overall ratios: 10·63, 7·7, 5·82 and 4·22 to 1. Final drive by 0·625 × 0·375-in chain. Mph at 1,000 rpm in top gear, 18.
Electrical Equipment: Coil ignition. 12-volt battery and dc dynamo. 6 in diameter headlamp with 45/35-watt main bulb. Starter motor; direction indicators; overload circuit breakers.
Brakes: Hydraulically-operated 10-in diameter duplex disc front, single disc rear.
Tyres: Goodyear Eagle A/T, 3·75 × 19-in front, 4·25 × 18-in rear, on cast-alloy wheels.
Suspension: Kayaba telescopic front fork. Pivoted rear fork with five-position spring preload adjustment.
Frame: Duplex tube cradle with cast lugs.
Dimensions: Wheelbase, 58·5 in; seat height, 31 in; handlebar width, 27 in; ground clearance, 8 in; all unladen.
Weight: 520 lb.
Fuel Capacity: approximately 2·5 UK gal (3 US gal)
Manufacturer: Harley-Davidson Motorcycles, 3700 West Juneau, Milwaukee, Wisconsin 53201.

Performance
Maximum Speeds (Mean): 115 mph (estimated); 100 mph (estimated) with rider normally seated.
Best One-way Speed: 115 mph (estimated).
Fuel Consumption: approximately 45 miles/UK gal (37 miles/US gal) overall.
Oil Consumption: approximately 500 mpp.
Minimum Non-snatch Speed: 15 mph in top gear.

mile warranty. Also new for the 1977 Harleys were Keihin carburettors made by the same firm that supplied Honda. The carburettor is a replica of the old simple Bendix unit with a single throttle valve and a massive choke button sprouting from the side.

Pull this, prime the combustion chambers from the carb's accelerator pump with a couple of twists of the grip, punch the big starter button on the handlebar and the big twin rumbles into life with its classic off-beat exhaust note from the black silencers.

From there on riding the bike is just a matter of letting the torque do the work. The clutch is heavy and the gearchange labourious so that once you snick into the highest of the four speeds there is rarely any need to change down, unless you stop at a light.

The overall gearing is very low with top gear giving just 3,900 rpm at 70 mph, a speed at which the Harley is no more than idling along. Tweak the grip and the bike, although fairly heavy at 520 lb, immediately kicks forward.

Through the four gears, flat out acceleration is brisk, but it is ragged and seems quicker than it really is. Nowadays a quarter-mile time of about 13 sec is only average for a 1,000 cc sports bike.

The top speed of 115 mph is similarly none too impressive, although faster than any other Harley made for the road. More pertinent however is the manner in which the performance is offered. Swinging through bends with the little footrests kissing the road, the syncopated note of the exhaust rebounding off the sidewalls, the XLCR becomes at one with the image that its appearance suggests. Such is the mystery and charm of such a machine, not the cold facts.

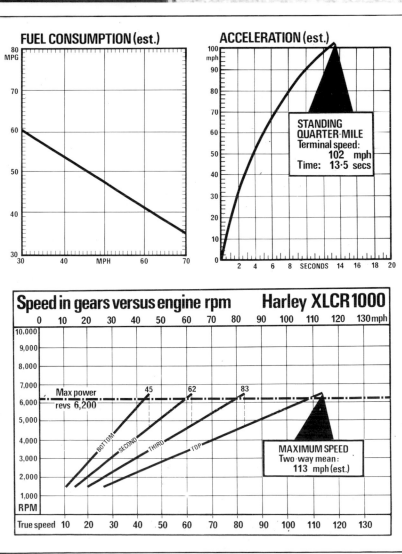

FUEL CONSUMPTION (est.)

ACCELERATION (est.)

STANDING QUARTER-MILE
Terminal speed: 102 mph
Time: 13·5 secs

Speed in gears versus engine rpm   Harley XLCR 1000

Max power revs 6,200

BOTTOM   SECOND   THIRD   TOP

MAXIMUM SPEED
Two-way mean:
113 mph (est.)

Honda CB750F2

Honda never let the grass grow under their feet. Quick to respond to changes in the market, as soon as their Super Sports 750 cc four was upstaged in performance and looks by Suzuki's GS750 four in late 1976, they quickly unveiled a new and even more potent model, the CB750F2.

The CB750F1 had been a positive effort by Honda to appeal to the purely sporting rider. Sharp styling and performance were allied to frame improvements to offer more stability at high speeds. It was the first effort by Honda in six years to change the image of a machine that had remained largely conservative in appearance since it started the superbike boom in 1969.

Menacingly resplendant with its all-black paintwork and engine set off by the five-spoke composite construction wheels based on the designs first used on the factory 1,000 cc endurance racers, the CB750F2 takes the sports theme further. Basically unchanged since it was introduced, the 736 cc overhead camshaft four-cylinder engine retains the same bore and stroke (61 × 63 mm) and the ruggedly reliable transmission with duplex primary chains taking the drive to the multiplate clutch and five-speed gearbox. Unusual by contemporary standards is the use of a countershaft behind the gearbox to take the drive to the final-drive sprocket.

For the F2, a retuning boosts the power and increases the rev band of the unit. Taking care of the higher power output is a heavier pitch endless rear chain with sealed links to improve life. Nevertheless, there are marks on the rear-wheel spindle mountings showing the amount of movement permissable before replacement is necessary. To marginally update the handling and high speed cornering stability there is new steering geometry, altered suspension settings and a tidier four-into-one exhaust system with greater ground clearance.

Where the F1 was capable of just over 120 mph, the F2 is a genuine 125 mph machine – and looks it. Equipment is first class. Mounted on the 'Comstar' wheels, which have stiff pressed-steel spokes and rolled light-alloy rims bolted to the hubs, are two brake discs at the front, with the single piston calipers mounted behind the fork legs, and a large diameter disc at the rear.

For night riding, the headlamp is a powerful quartz halogen unit, and there are two equally impressive horns mounted either side of it.

The 1976 CB750F1, the engine of which is now used in the same trim in the CB750K7, produced 67 bhp at 8,500 rpm. The CB750F2, by stretching the upper rev limit, gives more . . . 70 bhp at 9,500 rpm. This has been achieved by installing bigger valves and fitting the camshaft with a different profile. Inlet-valve sizes are increased from 32 to 34 mm, the exhausts from 28 to 31 mm, with stiffer springs (increased from 154 to 202 lb/in) to prevent valve float at the higher revs used. The long stroke motor can now be safely revved to over 10,000 rpm through the gears.

The larger valves called for a different valve angle and consequently there has been reshaping of the porting and of the combustion chamber, and a slight lowering of the compression ratio to prevent a broken marriage between the valves and pistons.

Looked at from a speed for speed's sake viewpoint the power boost produces the results. The bike takes off smoothly with a sharply determined power band starting at 6,000 rpm and goes like a jet up to the end of the rev counter's red sector, 10,500. The mean top speed of 124·6 mph reached is over 2 mph up on the F1 and puts the F2 up alongside its 1,000 cc stablemate, the GL1000 Gold Wing, in a flat-out match race. Given good conditions, the CB750F2 goes even better; with a tail wind it clocked a best speed of over 128 mph!

For everyday use, a marginal increase in valve clatter on tickover and a loss in tractability can be set against the power increase. For despite the drop in overall gearing (down to 5·51 to 1) minimum non-snatch speed of the F2 in top gear is 17 mph. The more flexible F1 accelerates more strongly in top gear and more cleanly from little over half that speed.

The loss shows in the standing quarter-mile times, too. The F1 zipped through at 13·2 seconds with a terminal speed of 100·9 mph. Despite more power and lower gearing the best we could get from the F2 was 13·5 seconds (but terminal speed was improved to almost 102 mph).

Feeding in the clutch and keeping the revs up gave the best result. Fitted with 242 lb/in springs in place of the 220 pounders used in 1976, the clutch withstood the punishment well and better than some earlier tests with 750 Honda engines when swelled plates necessitated adjustment.

Another contributory factor to the slower quarter-mile times is extra weight. For with the additional disc and caliper, horn, heavier duty chain and other modifications, weight is increased by 25 lb over the F1 tested in 1976.

Honda make amends with extra comfort and better fuel economy on the F2.

For the first time on a Honda 750 four, carburettors with enclosed lifters are used. Of the same choke size as the old models, 28 mm, the Keihin units sport accelerator pumps that allow the use of leaner overall jetting.

Pottering along at a steady 30 mph (33 indicated) the F3 returned a best figure of 80 mpg. Overall we averaged 45·3 mpg, an improvement on 1976. Provided the revs were used, the engine was quite happy on 3-star fuel; but lugging it below 5,000 rpm revealed a tendency for pinking.

The front fork, with a softer spring rate and modified damping valve arrangement, is the most comfortable and forgiving Honda have produced for the 750s so far, and with the new rear shocks few will find fault in the model's handling. This can become hairline at speed, but with nearly $4\frac{3}{4}$ inches of trail the steering is inevitably heavy and slightly cumbersome in filtering up to 20 mph through traffic. With the same frame as the F1, the F2 handlebars flutter slowing down through the 40–35 speed bracket, but there is little cause for concern. Few but cafe racers will find the need for further ground clearance with the four exhausts tucked neatly away into the high-mounted chrome silencer – one of the few items to escape the black paint treatment.

The silencer is particularly effective and makes the exhaust inaudible over the loud gearbox whine in third, fourth and top.

Going to the other extreme are the twin horns; this is a component regularly criticised by road testers in the past, irrespective of the make or model, but now it is changing. The effectiveness, by doubling up, has improved by leaps and bounds and the pair on the F2 made even the rider jump on the odd occasion they were needed. Similarly the brilliant Stanley halogen 60/65

watt headlight offers laser-like power compared to the older offerings. Set correctly, the sharp cut-off on dip prevents any chance of glare dazzling oncoming drivers or riders, while the vee-beam illuminates the kerb yards further ahead for safety. Once you have ridden at night behind the Honda's headlamp, or equivalent, you realise just what you are missing when you ride with second-rate equipment.

To cope with the extra power, and aiming for a longer life, a heavier duty $\frac{3}{4} \times \frac{3}{8}$-in endless drive

Specification
Engine: 736 cc (61 × 63 mm) single-overhead camshaft, transverse, in-line four. Five plain main bearings; plain big ends. Dry sump lubrication with trochoid pump; oil filter. Compression ratio, 9 to 1. Four 28-mm choke Keihin carburettors with accelerator pumps and cold-start flaps; paper-element air filter. Claimed maximum power, 70 bhp at 9,500 rpm.
Transmission: Duplex primary chain. Wet, multiplate clutch and five-speed gearbox. Overall ratios: 14·22, 9·72, 7·58, 6·45 and 5·51 to 1. Spur gears and endless 0·75 × 0·375-in drive chain (ratio 14/43).
Electrical Equipment: Coil ignition. 12-volt, 14-amp-hour battery and 210-watt alternator. 7-in diameter headlamp with 60/55-watt Stanley H4 quartz halogen main bulb. Starter motor; direction indicators; headlamp flasher and three fuses.
Brakes: Hydraulically-operated dual 11-in diameter stainless-steel disc front; single 12-in diameter disc rear.
Tyres: Bridgestone 3·25 × H19-in ribbed front; 4·00 × H18-in patterned rear.
Suspension: Telescopic front fork. Pivoted rear fork with five-position spring preload adjustment.
Frame: All welded, duplex cradle.
Dimensions: Wheelbase, 58·75 in; seat height, 32·5 in; ground clearance, 6·5 in; handlebar width, 28·5 in; castor angle, 62°30'; trail, 4·69 in; turning circle, 17 ft; all unladen.
Weight: 515 lb including one gallon of fuel.
Fuel Capacity: 4 UK gal (4·8 US gal).
Oil Capacity: 6 pt.
Manufacturer: Honda Motor Co. Ltd., 27-8, 6 Chome, Jingumae, Shibuya-ku, Tokyo.

Performance
Maximum Speeds (Mean): 124·6 mph; 108·4 mph with rider sitting normally.
Best One-way Speed: 128·4 mph – dry track, light tail wind.
Braking Distance – from 30 mph: 28 ft 3 in.
Fuel Consumption: 45·3 miles/UK gal (37·7 miles/US gal) overall.
Oil Consumption: Negligible.
Minimum Non-snatch Speed: 17 mph in top gear.
Speedo Accuracy:

Indicated mph	30	40	50	60	70	80	90	100
Actual mph	26·9	36·0	45·1	54·3	63·5	74·3	83·6	94·4

Honda's long standing four-cylinder single overhead camshaft CB750 sported 'Comstar' wheels with pressed-steel spokes and light alloy rims for 1977. Engine power was boosted to 70 bhp at 9,000 rpm with new carburettors, camshaft and larger valves

chain replaces the former $\frac{5}{8} \times \frac{3}{8}$-in chain. Each bearing is packed with grease at manufacture and sealed in by rubber O-rings. It is very effective and only needed re-tensioning by a third of a turn of the spindle adjusters in 600 test miles.

The F1 with its single disc was never short on stopping power, and braking is even more impressive with the F2's two discs on the front wheel. Sensibly each stainless-steel disc is thinner than the single, to help save unsprung weight, and the calipers are mounted to the rear of the fork reducing the steering inertia. Disc pads, the same all round, are now slotted to improve wet weather performance.

With a stopping distance from 30 mph of 28ft 3in, the tyres now handicap stopping in even shorter distances – with such a potent front brake the tyre loses adhesion without much provocation. With the nose pinned down the rider should tread lightly on the rear brake, for if anything the new 12-in diameter disc is too much brake for the job.

The Comstar wheels, so radically different from spoked or cast-alloy jobs, meet with immediate approval. They are very strong, suit the concept and enhance the looks of the F2 – if anything they are progressively winning over their opponents as they become more familiar and accepted. Setbacks, if you approve of their looks, are poorer accessibility for cleaning between the five 'spokes' compared with the cast-alloy type; and similarly they cannot be trued like a normal spoked wheel after a minor shunt.

With little bright relief offered by a maroon petrol tank and side panels, it is up to the wheels, chromed exhaust, clutch and contact-breaker covers, and alloy generator cover, to provide contrast. This Honda have achieved with boldness and taste on the F2.

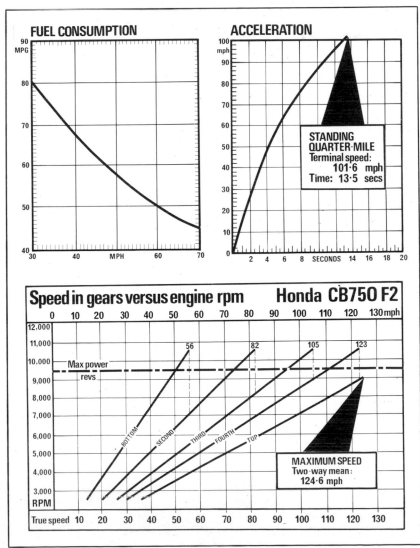

FUEL CONSUMPTION

ACCELERATION

STANDING QUARTER-MILE
Terminal speed: 101·6 mph
Time: 13·5 secs

Speed in gears versus engine rpm — Honda CB750 F2

MAXIMUM SPEED
Two-way mean: 124·6 mph

Honda Gold Wing GL1000

If there is one machine that typifies American motor cycling and the fact that it is essentially different from biking in Europe it is the Honda Gold Wing. Without justification, this has been described as a two-wheeled tank, or more mildly as a car without bodywork. In fact few bikes can equal the Gold Wing for luxurious high-speed cruising.

It was designed with the Stateside tourer expressly in mind. What he wanted was a bike that could cover massive mileages without trouble on the open freeways that span the North American continent. He wanted a machine that could carry enormous amounts of luggage as well as a passenger.

Few bikes, if any, could satisfy Americans completely in these aspects. Those which were offered were often unreliable or expensive. What

Honda introduced in 1974 was the biggest and heaviest machine ever marketed by the Japanese company. And it was the bike that the Americans wanted. Utterly quiet, as smooth as silk and trouble free with its shaft drive, it came at a price that undercut the opposition by as much as 25 per cent. It was an immediate success. It was also a revolutionary motor cycle.

Barely a couple of years earlier, nobody would have thought that soon there would be a water-cooled horizontally opposed flat four on the market at a price that anybody could afford. But here it was, and it was not the monster that everybody expected.

Honda had to make the machine manageable at low speeds, or it could have been a complete flop, so they designed the bike with the concentration of heaviest parts as low as possible in the

frame. To this end the gearbox is beneath the crankshaft, a bonus being that the engine is shorter too. Helping to reduce the centre of gravity, the fuel tank is mounted under the rider's seat, the dummy tank being used to house the air filter, the electrics, the overflow tank for the engine coolant and a small tool tray. Remarkably, the bike steers very well and is a lot more manageable than one might expect of a machine weighing 650 lb with a full tank, which is almost 100 lb more than the Kawasaki Z1000. Despite its bulk and very high gearing it is surprisingly fast for what is basically a touring bike.

It has of course been pushed out of the limelight by more recent big machines from Yamaha and Suzuki, but no machine has been able to give the feel of the iron fist in the velvet glove as effectively.

From idling revs to 8,000 rpm the power is developed in a smooth continuous stream. The only vibration, and it could hardly be called that, exists when you shut off or when pulling hard from a walking pace in top gear.

The impression of speed, since the only sounds the engine makes are muted clicks and whines, comes from wind pressure and roar.

Cruising at 100 mph is completely natural for the Gold Wing. It whistles along with plenty in hand and with total stability. Theoretically, the bike is capable of 140 mph on the top gear ratio of 4·5 to 1. But this is really too high and, in practice, the actual top speed is around 125 mph as we found at our MIRA tests. Straight line acceleration is stunning too, and the Wing's 80 bhp at 7,500 rpm gently wafts you to over 60 mph in 4 sec and 100 mph in a shade over 13 sec. The lazy sounding engine achieves this with a distinct lack of commotion. Apart from the four 32-mm choke carburettors between the crankcases and the dummy tank, it has more in common with car power units than bike engines.

The four 72-mm cylinders (stroke is 61·4 mm) have wet liners and are pressed into the two halves of the crankcases which are split vertically. Light-alloy cylinder heads have offset valves and overhead camshafts driven by toothed belts from the front end. The left-hand camshaft also drives the contact breaker, while the fuel pump is driven by the right-hand camshaft.

Cleverly, the 300-watt alternator is gear-driven from the crankshaft so that its opposed motion offsets the in-line crank and minimises the reaction when the revs rise and fall quickly.

Transmission from the crank is by a Morse-type chain to the wet, multiplate clutch (a very sensitive unit that dislikes excessive slipping) and the slick and crisp-acting five-speed gearbox. An idler gear takes the drive to a spring torsion damper and the drive shaft inside the right-hand fork leg to the rear wheel and spiral-bevel gears.

Inevitably, the first impression of the machine is its overwhelming bulk. The wheelbase is 61 inches and if the dummy tank were real it would hold at least 7 gallons. But the seat is low, if a little hard, and reaching the ground with the feet is easy for any but the shorter rider.

Pulling the car-type choke button next to the speedo and rev counter and pressing the starter button next to the twistgrip immediately has the engine running at 3,000 rpm from cold. No juggling with the throttle is called for as the

The Honda Gold Wing's water-cooled flat four owes more to car practice than motor cycles. The overhead camshafts are driven by toothed belts and the gearbox is beneath the crankshaft.
Far right: electrics, air filter and a tool tray are inside the dummy tank. The rear fuel tank is under the seat

Specification

Engine: 1000 cc (72 × 61·4 mm) overhead camshaft, water-cooled, opposed flat four. Light-alloy cylinder heads, steel linered cylinders integral with crankcase. Three plain main bearings; plain big ends. Wet sump lubrication. Compression ratio, 9·2 to 1. Four 32-mm Mikuni constant-velocity carburettors with handle-bar operated cold start flaps; paper element air filter. Claimed maximum power, 80 bhp at 7,500 rpm.

Transmission: Inverted-tooth primary chain. Wet, multiplate clutch and five-speed gearbox beneath crankshaft. Overall ratios: 11·98, 8·18, 6·39, 5·25 and 4·5 to 1. Final drive by reduction gear from layshaft and cardan shaft. Mph at 1,000 rpm in top gear, 17.

Electrical Equipment: Twin coil ignition. 12-volt, 18-amp-hour battery and contra rotating, 300-watt alternator and voltage regulator. 7-in diameter Lucas headlamp with 60/55-watt halogen bulb. Direction indicators; starter motor; water-temperature gauge; electric fuel gauge; headlamp flasher.

Brakes: Hydraulically-operated 11-in diameter duplex disc front, 11·5-in diameter single rear.

Tyres: Dunlop Gold Seal, 3·50 × H19-in ribbed front, 4·50 × H17-in studded rear. Light-alloy rims.

Suspension: Telescopic front fork. Pivoted rear fork with five-position spring preload adjustment.

Frame: Duplex tube with pressed-steel gusseting and removable left-hand side bottom rail for engine access.

Dimensions: Wheelbase, 60·5 in; ground clearance, 6 in; seat height, 31·5 in; overall length, 91 in; turning circle, 17 ft; all unladen.

Weight: 618 lb.

Fuel Capacity: 4·2 UK gal (5 US gal) including 6 pt reserve.

Sump Oil Capacity: 6·2 pt.

Manufacturer: Honda Motor Co. Ltd, 27-8, 6 Chome, Jingumae, Shibuya-ku, Tokyo.

Performance

Maximum Speeds (Mean): 124·6 mph; 111·4 mph with rider in two-piece outfit sitting normally.

Best One-way Speed: 130 mph – dry track, strong tail wind.

Braking Distance – from 30 mph: 29 ft.

Fuel Consumption: 41·6 miles/UK gal (34·5 miles/US gal) overall.

Oil Consumption: negligible.

Minimum Non-snatch Speed: 17 mph in top gear.

Speedo Accuracy:

Indicated mph	30	40	50	60	70	80	90	100
Actual mph	29·2	39·5	49·7	58·7	67·8	77·6	87·4	97·2

complex choke mechanism opens the flaps a shade to keep the revs steady.

The engine is ready for work almost instantly. The pressurised water-cooling system warms up quickly with the aid of a thermostat and within a few minutes the needle of the temperature gauge in the rev counter face creeps to the bottom of its range.

From then on the only attention the beast requires is regular refilling with fuel. Despite its weight, the Gold Wing can be economical, particularly as it runs on the cheapest grade of fuel. Over 1,000 miles of testing it averaged 42 mpg, with a slightly better consumption on motorways.

This gives a range of about 145 miles before the fuel gauge on the top of the dummy tank shows empty, giving roughly 40 miles more on the six pint reserve capacity. Ideally, a bike like this should have a range of 200 miles before running onto reserve.

The riding position is acceptable, although not in the BMW class because of the excessive reach to the handlebar.

Given the Gold Wing's market, its handling is beyond criticism. Ridden in the reserved fashion that one would expect of a tourer, it corners steadily if with a slight 'fall-in' effect under 30 mph and is manageable in traffic, more so than many European machines. But it is not a sporting machine and if ridden as such will bite the rider hard, which is why the Wing has received so much criticism from Europeans.

The fold up footrests are very low and like the enormous exhaust system that wraps around the rear wheel, are easily scraped on the road when cornering briskly.

The suspension is harsh too, detracting from the ride quality at normal cruising speeds, and the damping is less than adequate when the bike is pushed hard through bumpy bends. There are things that cannot be done with a 650 lb motor cycle, and it cannot be made to feel like a lightweight when the pace gets hot. The rider must remember that he has very little room for maneuovre when riding fast.

Wet weather riding shows up some good and some bad features of the bike. Riding at speed, the rider is well protected from water spray by the well valanced front mudguard and cooling radiator. But the brakes are not well protected – normally, the stoppers, two front stainless steel discs and one rear, are powerful and progressive, but in wet weather, particularly at slow speeds in town and when drenched on motorways, the discs lack any sort of bite at all. The only recourse for the rider is to dab the brakes periodically to keep them dry. Hopefully Honda will soon have an answer to this braking problem.

The electrical system is up to the usual standard expected from Honda and enhanced by the powerful quartz halogen headlamp.

The Gold Wing is a sensible and cheaper alternative to the 980 cc BMW twins. In a straight line it is probably better and the gear change on the Honda is definitely superior. The quality of construction that dictates the higher price of the BMW is reflected only in better handling, appearance and durability. The same goes for the Guzzis which also have shaft drive. The competition will take a long time to come up with a bike as good as the Honda at the same price.

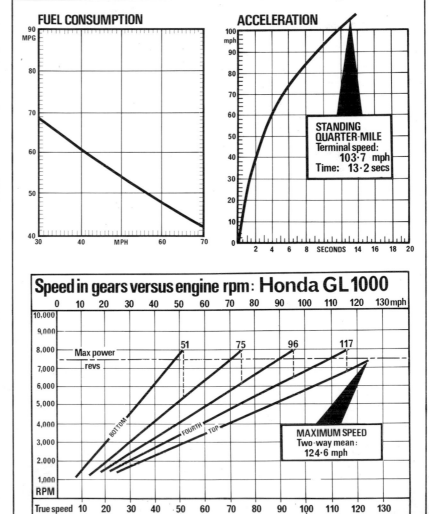

FUEL CONSUMPTION

ACCELERATION

STANDING QUARTER-MILE
Terminal speed: 103·7 mph
Time: 13·2 secs

Speed in gears versus engine rpm: Honda GL1000

Max power revs

BOTTOM FOURTH TOP

MAXIMUM SPEED
Two-way mean: 124·6 mph

Kawasaki Z650

Kawasaki's Z650 four has carved itself an enviable reputation for speed and stamina since it appeared in late 1976. Proof of the speed came at Daytona in the following March when Kawasaki attacked the world 750 cc endurance records with a trio of mildly modified Z650 roadsters. They came away with a bunch of records that would have been impressive for a 1,000 cc roadster, let alone a 650. Best were the FIM world 1,000 km at 128·4 mph, the AMA/FIM six-hour at 127·7 mph and the AMA 100-miler at 130 mph. For good measure they rounded off with the world FIM 24-hour record at 117·2 mph. Earlier, the American, Rich Willet attacked the round the coast Australia record on his Z650 with a colleague. Just over ten days later he was back at Sydney having covered 9,550 miles to beat the record for the toughest trip in motor cycling by the scant margin of one hour. This was despite the 44-year old St Louis businessman spending a day helping his companion to hospital after a crash and after side-swiping a kangaroo hard enough for Rich to think he had broken a leg. The Z650 never missed a beat.

We were not quite so adventurous during our own 600-mile road test but we learned that those records were no fluke. Firstly, there is no doubt that the Z650 is very fast. It can accelerate to 60 mph as quick as anything you can buy on wheels. If proof was ever needed that there is only one thing better than a fast big bike, and that's a fast small bike, the Z650 is it.

For motor cycles, small is definitely beautiful. If there is one thing that hampers the enjoyment of a bike, it is weight and bulk. The bulkier and heavier a machine the more difficult it is to manoeuvre, the more trouble it becomes when cornering and the more fuel it uses.

The Z650 Kawasaki is tangible evidence that smaller is better. At 495 lb, it weighs some 30 lb

lighter than most of the seven fifties and with a 56½-in wheelbase is about 3 inches shorter. On the road the bike gives away nothing in performance and is far and away a better performer than 550 cc machines. Flat-out mean top speed at MIRA was 119·6 mph, only 4 mph down on Suzuki's GS750 and 2 mph less than the Honda CB750F1.

Even more stunning is its acceleration. Taking to the test track like a drag racer, the Z650 scorched through the quarter-mile in 12·9 sec with a terminal speed of 101·6 mph. Although eight runs were timed, six of which were 13 sec or under, the bike finished as unruffled as ever.

The secret is not only the power of the twin-cam 652 cc short-stroke, four-cylinder engine, but the bike's perfect gearing and balance. The Z650's wheelbase is neither so short as to provoke unmanageable wheelies on take-off nor so long that there is too much wheelspin.

Drop the clutch at 7,000 rpm and the Kawasaki just digs in and gets on with the job, the front wheel just hovering above the tarmac for the first few yards. It is as though the bike was made for drag racing. The proof of this is that the Z650 is one of the quickest bikes from rest through 110 yards. The terminal speed of 66·8 mph has only been beaten once – by the super-fast 1973 Kawasaki Z1 903 cc four at 68 mph. It can reach 50 mph in just 3 sec from rest.

Yet the bike is no awkward rev-happy racer. Although it can scream up to 10,000 rpm (the red line is at 9,000 rpm), the engine is sweet and flexible enough to haul along at under 4,000 rpm and there is torque enough to give a sizeable kick in the seat as you open up.

Apart from a band around 7,000 rpm, the Z650 is exceptionally smooth for a four in-line, particularly at about 70 mph in top gear (equal to 5,500 rpm.) This makes it very relaxing to ride at speed, particularly as there is hardly a hint of 'cammyness' with ample response throughout the range.

Power characteristics like this usually result in above average fuel economy, but although the six-fifty four could return 52 mpg around town, the overall test figure of 46·5 mpg was lower than expected, but doubtless due to the heavy consumption of 34 mpg during the performance testing. Range on the 3½ gallon fuel tank is between 150 and 160 miles.

Although Kawasaki claim the machine will run on unleaded fuel like the Z1000, in the case of the test bike unless it was run on four-star fuel it would detonate at small throttle openings when pulling hard. This off-idle weakness in the mixture strength was probably connected with the Z650's excessive cold-bloodedness when starting from cold. The process of starting is made more tricky by the need to disengage the clutch when pressing the starter button.

Excellent though the machine is on the track or when ridden hard, the Z650 is not quite so impressive when the going is more relaxed. At low speeds, for example around town streets, the gearchange hangs up and is very clunky, particularly when engaging bottom gear from neutral. On the open road, the gearbox which is identical to the unit on the Z750 twin, is by contrast as slick and crisp as you could want.

Town riding is further spoiled by the excessive backlash in the gearbox, which is compounded by that stuttering in the carburation.

Being much smaller and more compact than the Z1000, the Z650 has none of the bigger model's awe-inspiring bulk, and it is a markedly better handling machine. Although the sus-

pension is softer and more comfortable than the big model one can skim through bends much more confidently than the Z900 or Z1000 would ever allow, and with none of the gut-churning high-speed wobbles that still mark the Z1000 as a bike to be respected when the going gets hot.

The main improvement on the Z650 is a stiffer frame with more sensibly designed steering geometry. The rake of the front fork has been pulled back to 63 degrees, in line with the Z750

twin, and combined with more trail. The bike is very stable in fast bends, while at low speeds there is only the slightest hint of 'oversteer' – that feeling that the bike wants to drop further into a corner – and unlike the Z900 it does not want to straighten up when cranked over in fast corners.

Ground clearance is enhanced by use of one silencer either side and the only limitation on the amount you can crank the bike over is the grip of the Dunlop Gold Seal tyres. If you manage to touch down the left side projection of the main stand you are a long, long way over.

Harder riders will prefer stiffer springs on the Z650, for although it is very much a sporting bike, the suspension has been tailored to have a broader appeal. The 100 lb/in rear springs give a smooth ride and the dampers are fairly well matched – like the front fork.

However, there is still some of the vagueness in the overall feel of the machine that puts it not quite on par with the best handling roadsters now available.

Like the GS750 Suzuki, the Z650 has been well planned for the rider. The seat is soft yet secure enough to prevent you moving about, and the footrests are well tucked in.

The lowish handlebar is properly swept back at the right angle and can be adjusted to taste even though the wiring runs neatly through the tubing. Only general criticism of the Z650 is that the shortness of the bike will put off taller riders. Cruising at anything over 70 mph becomes tiresome after only a few minutes due to the height of the handlebar grips.

Along with practically all other Japanese bikes the Z650 has a stainless-steel, front-brake disc which is fine when dry, but always has to be allowed for when wet and cold. Kawasaki sensibly resisted the fashionable temptation to fit another to the rear wheel, and retain a 7-in drum brake. This works admirably, the brakes being neither too grabby nor under-powered.

Electrical equipment, apart from the head-lamp, is first class. A high power 280-watt alternator supplies all the needs of the system and

Specification

Engine: 652 cc (62 × 54 mm) double overhead camshaft, transverse, in-line four. Light-alloy cylinder block and head. Five plain main bearings; plain big ends. Wet sump lubrication; Eaton-type pump. Compression ratio, 9·5 to 1. Four Mikuni 24-mm choke carburettors with lever-operated cold-start jets; paper element air filter. Maximum claimed power, 64 bhp at 8,500 rpm; maximum torque, 42 lb-ft at 7,000 rpm.

Transmission: Primary inverted-tooth chain and spur gears. Wet, multiplate clutch and five-speed gearbox. Overall ratios: 15·6, 10·9, 8·5, 6·96 and 5·95 to 1. Final drive by endless 0·625 × 0·375-in chain. Mph at 1,000 rpm in top gear, 12·8.

Electrical Equipment: Twin coil ignition. 12-volt, 10-amp-hour battery and 280-watt field-excited alternator. 7-in diameter headlamp with 45/40-watt main bulb. Starter motor; four fuses.

Brakes: Hydraulically-operated 11·75-in diameter stainless-steel disc front with single piston floating caliper; 7-in diameter drum rear.

Tyres: Dunlop Gold Seal, 3·25 × 19-in F6 ribbed front, 4·00 × 18-in patterned K87 rear.

Suspension: Telescopic front fork. Pivoted rear fork with five-position spring preload adjustment.

Frame: All-welded duplex tube cradle with triple spine tubes.

Dimensions: Wheelbase, 56·5 in; seat height, 32 in; ground clearance, 6·5 in; handlebar width, 29 in; castor angle, 63°; trail, 4·25 in; turning circle, 15 ft 6 in; all unladen.

Weight: 495 lb including one gallon of fuel.

Fuel Capacity: 3·7 UK gal (4·4 US gal) including reserve.

Sump Oil Capacity: 6·2 pt.

Manufacturer: Kawasaki Heavy Industries (Engine and Motorcycle Group), 1-1 Kawasaki-cho, Akashi-city, Hyogo Pref., Japan.

Performance

Maximum Speeds (Mean): 119·6 mph; 102·7 mph with rider in two-piece oversuit sitting normally.

Best One-way Speed: 121·2 mph – dry track, three-quarter tail wind.

Braking Distance – from 30 mph: 29 ft 3 in.

Fuel Consumption: 46·5 miles/UK gal (38·6 miles/US gal) overall.

Oil Consumption: 1,000 mpp overall.

Minimum Non-snatch Speed: 15 mph in top gear.

Speedo Accuracy:

Indicated mph	30	40	50	60	70	80	90
Actual mph	28·6	37·4	46·2	55·8	63·3	73·8	84·3

Control layout of the Z650 shows the standard Japanese approach with dipswitch, direction indicator switches, horn button and headlamp flasher on the left and light switch, cut out and starter button on the right. Note that the mirrors are too narrow; they should be at least 2 in wider

The Z650 is a classic example of contemporary Japanese engineering with double overhead cams, short stroke, an all plain bearing crankshaft and drive to the five-speed gearbox by means of a Morse-type chain and jackshaft

the battery never went limp after days of slow commuter riding. Indicators are large and bright. However, the headlamp suffers from being indistinct and lacking in penetration on both dipped and main beam.

The heart of the Z650 is its modern power unit. Quiet and unobtrusive, it whispers along with hardly a rustle from the valve gear or exhaust. At 70 mph in top the engine is barely audible above wind roar. Designed specifically with quietness in mind, it shares more in common with Honda's CB500 four. Unlike the Z1000 with its roller bearing crankshaft and gear primary drive, the Z650 uses a plain bearing crank with a Morse type chain running to a shaft between the crank and the clutch, which is driven by gears. For longevity, the valves are opened by twin-overhead camshafts and bucket followers and although the Kawasaki service book says that valve clearances need checking every 3,000 miles, it is claimed that they will not need attention until four times that distance. That is just as well, for the camshafts need to be lifted to vary the 47p shims under the buckets.

Longer servicing intervals are becoming more and more common; details like the sight window on the engine to check oil level ease the work. The rear chain, although very costly, pays its way by lasting up to 700 miles before needing adjustment thanks to the use of O-rings to keep the oil in the links – and the dirt out.

Undoubtedly, the Z650 is the best Kawasaki so far. It restores the image of thundering power and speed with a new one of civilised restraint. The Z650 can afford to be sober in appearance because it takes on the 750s and just about equals them at their own game.

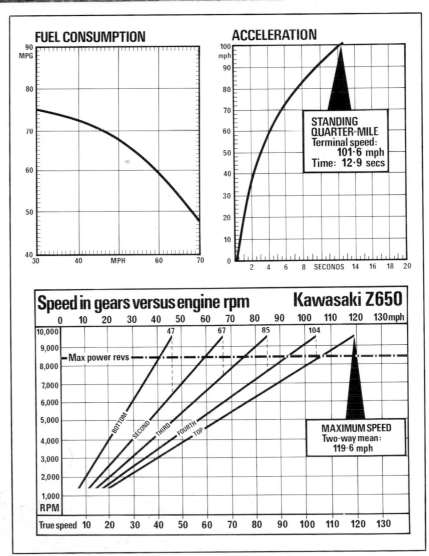

FUEL CONSUMPTION

ACCELERATION

STANDING QUARTER-MILE
Terminal speed: **101·6 mph**
Time: **12·9 secs**

Speed in gears versus engine rpm   **Kawasaki Z650**

MAXIMUM SPEED
Two-way mean: **119·6 mph**

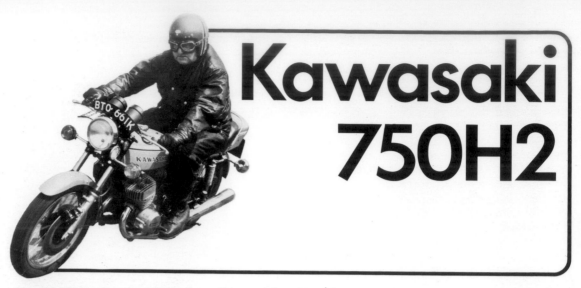

Kawasaki 750H2

Along with the Honda CB750 four, Kawasaki's Mach III 500 cc three-cylinder two-stroke was the precursor of the fabulous range of superbikes available today. But unlike the Honda, which came out a year earlier, the 1969 Mach III was a no-holds-barred speedster with few concessions to comfort, civility or good handling. With its white finish and three pipes jutting to the rear, it was the ultimate two-wheel hot rod; sharp models could break the quarter mile beams in under 13 sec and top 120 mph flat out.

So when Kawasaki showed the 750 cc version early in 1972, the motor cycling world gasped in disbelief; if the 500 cc three had an exceptional performance for its time, the seven fifty was going to be *unreal*.

It was. Crammed into the lightest motor cycle in the seven fifty class was the most bristly engine ever seen from Japan. Three 250 cc air-cooled cylinders sat side-by-side across the frame and bulged out either side. Before the days when it was necessary to heed the noise levels, the Mach IV as it was first called, clattered and jangled. But no matter, it really was powerful, with a claimed 74 bhp at 6,500 rpm.

It was only when the even bigger 900 cc Kawasaki four-stroke four was introduced a little later that the 750 three was trounced in the power stakes.

Yet even then its time was limited – the introduction of the four-stroke Kawasaki was the writing on the wall. For all its smokey, gas-guzzling and exciting performance, the 750's supreme grossness could not be tolerated for ever. After all, a brisk rider could empty the fuel tank at a rate that made the air vent whistle on the cap; 20 mpg was nothing unusual for this supreme example of one-dimensional travel. Inevitably, there was no 750 cc three in the 1976 Kawasaki range, its place ably taken by the more civil but no less potent Z650 dohc four.

Even so, its fans still look back to those hazy days when you could whip up the front wheel with no more than a tweak at the grip. Just careful tuning of the motor would be rewarded with 12·2 sec standing quarters and terminal speeds around 110 mph.

Yet for all its getaway potential, the big

Kwacker was city-trained. It could be eased away gently from a traffic halt. It would chug along in the highest of its five ratios at under 30 mph. It did not oil up its plugs. And it stood out in a crowd. The finish was bright blue, with coloured stripes along the tank and tail pressings. Engine castings were brightly polished; three long, uptilted silencers glittered in the sunlight. The appeal was irresistible.

The maximum speed of anything so exotic as the seven-fifty Kawasaki may be of largely academic interest in this speed-limited world. Taking into account a top gear ratio of 4·76 to 1, and a maximum power figure at 6,800 rpm, the Mach IV was geared for a theoretical top speed of 111 mph. But with the rider in racing leathers and flat down to it, and with the revmeter needle well past the 7,000 blood-line on the dial, we got a two-way mean of 115 mph, with a best-one-way (helped, to a small extent, by a three-quarter crosswind) of 117 mph.

Unlike many other high-performance two-strokes, the greater part of the urge of the Mach IV is not confined to a narrow band high up the rev scale. Instead, there is a reasonable flow of power that begins early on, to give acceptable driveability for traffic work.

When one talks of two-stroke multis, the immediate thought is of a super-silkiness, a turbine-like smoothness. But with the Kawasaki, there was a slight vibration, felt through one's boot soles, at 5,000 rpm; with the revmeter needle in the red patch at 7,000 rpm, the tingling extended to the fingers.

No electric starter was fitted. Instead, there was a very long, folding starter pedal which was easy to use. The wakey-wakey procedure also called for action on the starter-jet thumb lever, located near the twistgrip. The lever is a shade awkward to reach, but it needed to be held down for the first couple of seconds. Thereafter, some adroit juggling of twistgrip, thumb lever and clutch lever was necessary until the engine was warmed up enough to face the hurly-burly of another new day. Usually, that was by the time it reached the top of the street. With the engine already hot there was no need for more than one swing on the pedal.

Well in advance of the introduction of the model in Europe, hair-raising rumours about heavy fuel consumption had been wafted across the Atlantic. Well, it has always been a truism that, with a two-stroke engine especially, speed must be paid for; and the bigger the unit, the heavier the bill.

When the throttle was treated gingerly, the outcome was not too unreasonable. At a steady 30 mph, for example, the consumption worked out at around 56 mpg. But when the throttle hand gets itchy, the three carburettors just open their throats and the consumption increases rather alarmingly.

For those who could afford the H2, perhaps its fuel consumption of 25 mpg at 70 mph was neither here nor there. A snag was that the 3¾-gallon tank had to be filled up frequently.

As supplied, brand-new, the Mach IV was equipped with the high and wide Western-style handlebar. For the 1,000-mile running-in period, this bar was persevered with but, before the performance-test session, the bike was returned to the importers for a check-over, and a short flat handlebar (from the Mach III five-hundred, in fact) was substituted. The flat bar could be fitted by the importers (Agrati Sales) if the customer asked for it.

In addition, at the tester's request, the hydraulically-operated auxiliary steering damper was detached. The damper was an extra and hinders rather than helps in low-speed running.

The changeover was not entirely a matter of personal preference. With the high bar, the dead upright riding position was comfortable enough once one had become used to it, but it seemed more suited for a gentle amble up and down the seafront on a sunny day, than for serious motor cycling. Moreover, on a couple of occasions at around 80 mph, a slow roll developed.

With the flat bar, the transformation was dramatic. Here was a totally different motor cycle, far more purposeful, far more comfortable

Business as usual for the Kawasaki 750 two-stroke three. These are the sort of antics that would reward a twitchy right wrist. The super fast Kwacker was a surprise example of the early Seventies superbike

for high-speed work, and, above all, one which had acquired rock-steady stability. Now the bike could be bent into corners with complete peace of mind.

The three-cylinder engine is undoubtedly wide, but it is set high in the frame so there is no fear of any part of it grounding when cornering.

Throughout the test, the rear damper units were set at the softest of the three settings. This proved to be adequate, even with a 220 lb rider and a 170 lb pillion passenger added for good measure.

Although fairly firm, the saddle did not become uncomfortably hard on a long ride. But the Kawasaki appeared to have been designed with long-leg six-footers in mind; it is possible – almost – for an average-size rider to reach the ground firmly with both feet, but an inch off the existing seat height would have been appreciated.

A sticking clutch is not normally experienced with Japanese two-strokes, but the big Kawasaki had it in full measure. Before switching on the ignition for the first start of the day, it was highly desirable to hold in the clutch lever while giving the kickstarter two or three hefty jabs to free the plates. If this routine was neglected, the result was a lurch forward, stalling the engine, as soon as the pedal was moved into bottom gear.

Even with the plate-freeing ritual observed, bottom-gear engagement produced a very definite clonk, but from then on pedal movement was crisp and short, the dogs sliding into mesh quietly and easily.

Unlike its sisters in the Kawasaki range, the Mach IV had its neutral position below bottom gear. This arrangement has the advantage that neutral is invariably easy to select, but on the other hand there is always the chance of overriding bottom when engine braking is wanted.

Because the engine pulls well from low rpm, there is no need to cane the clutch on getaway. Take-up is light and sweet and in everyday use no adjustment was needed. However, in obtaining standing-quarter-mile and acceleration-test figures, the plates did become overheated. After a cooling-off period of a few minutes, cable clearance returned to normal, and the tests could continue.

A chain oiler was fitted. This takes the form of a drip feed to the top run of the rear chain, but it works only when a spring-loaded knob is held up, while at the same time the rear wheel is spun by hand. The business is rather tedious, and is only a slight improvement over using a squirt oil-can.

Headlamp main-beam lighting could hardly be better; it was brilliant and far-reaching. Perhaps its brightness made one more than usually conscious of the loss of illumination when the dip beam was brought into use. The cut-off was flat and did its job of preventing dazzle very well, and the beam was broad enough to show up the sides of the road, but the drop in candle power was too marked for comfort.

The headlamp switch and the dipswitch are in a cluster on the left of the handlebar, and are nicely placed for use with a gloved hand. In the same cluster is the direction-indicator switch; here, too, the positioning is just right. The indicator switch had an easy action – perhaps too easy, for one often over-corrected when flicking to the off position.

Speedometer and revmeter dials were prominent and easy to read, with green figures on a black background. Both instruments are excellently illuminated, in such a way that they can be read after dark without the rider's attention being distracted from the road ahead. The face of the revmeter also incorporates an amber repeater light for the direction indicators, and a green neutral-indicator light. The indicator beacons themselves are big and bright, and readily seen by other road-users.

The only dull note on the electrical side came from the horn, which emitted a tired bleep rather out of character with a potent seven-fifty.

The front brake is an 11-in diameter disc. Movement at the handlebar lever was relatively slight, but the brake provides ample sensitivity. In average running it was necessary only to caress the lever with a couple of fingers to obtain gentle retardation; even a crash stop did not require excessive lever pressure.

The 8-in diameter drum brake at the rear was slightly spongy in operation. Nevertheless, when used in conjunction with the front disc the bike could be stopped in 25 ft 6 in, from a steady 30 mph, on dry tarmac. This performance was repeated time and again, with no falling-off in consistency. On wet roads, the rear brake would

Specification

Engine: 748 cc (71 × 63 mm) transverse, in-line, two-stroke three. Light-alloy cylinder barrels and heads. Crankshaft supported in six ball bearings; needle-roller big ends and small ends. Injectolube automatic lubrication, feeding into intake tracts, and to main and big-end bearings. Three Mikuni VM30SC 30-mm choke carburettors; paper-element air filter. Claimed maximum power, 74 bhp at 6,800 rpm.

Transmission: Primary by spur gears through wet, multiplate clutch to all-indirect, five-speed gearbox. Overall ratios: 12·76, 8·64, 6·53, 5·31 and 4·76 to 1. Final drive by 0·625 × 0·375-in chain. Engine rpm at 30 mph in top gear, 1,850 rpm.

Electrical Equipment: Ignition by 12-volt, 6-amp-hour battery and three coils. Charging by 150-watt alternator, through rectifier and voltage regulator. 7-in diameter headlamp with 35/25-watt main bulb. Direction indicators.

Brakes: Hydraulically-operated 11-in diameter disc front, 7·9-in diameter drum rear.

Tyres: Yokohama, 3·25 × 19 in ribbed front, 4·00 × 18-in studded rear.

Suspension: Hydraulically-damped telescopic front fork; pivoted rear fork controlled by spring-and-hydraulic struts with three-position adjustment for load.

Frame: Duplex loop cradle.

Dimensions: Wheelbase, 55 in; seat height, 32 in; ground clearance, 8 in; turning circle, 15 ft 6 in; all unladen.

Weight: 432 lb with approximately 1·5 gallons of fuel and 2 pt of oil.

Fuel Capacity: 3·75 UK gal (4·5 US gal) including about 6 pt reserve.

Oil Tank Capacity: 3·5 pt.

Manufacturer: Kawasaki Heavy Industries (Engine and Motorcyle Group), Hammamatsu, Japan.

Performance

Maximum Speed (Mean): 115 mph.
Best One-way Speed: 117 mph – dry track, moderate three-quarter wind.
Braking Distance – from 30 mph: 25 ft 6 in on dry tarmac.
Fuel Consumption: 33 miles/UK gal (27·4 miles/US gal) at 60 mph.
Minimum Non-snatch Speed: 24 mph in top gear.

lock the wheel very readily – probably because the Yokohama tyres did not give as much grip as other makes.

No mere decoration, the pressed-steel tailpiece houses a kit with a selection of good-quality tools, including pliers. There was room, also, to include a pint can of oil.

Apart from one adjustment of the rear chain, there was no need to open the tool kit in anger during the period the bike was in our hands.

Engine accessibility is good, with for example, contact-breaker points and oil pump concealed behind covers retained by easy-to-remove screws. Taking out the front wheel presented fewer difficulties than with a conventional drum brake – no cable or torque arm to disconnect. All that is necessary is to detach the fork-end caps.

Removing the rear wheel is another matter. The chain has no detachable link, so the adjusters must be slackened right off and the wheel pushed forward, to allow the chain to be peeled off the sprocket. (Unlike its smaller sisters, the seven-fifty does not have a quickly detachable rear hub, and although there is a pull-out spindle, its head is on the right, where it is screened completely by the twin silencers which, therefore, must first be detached.)

As with most present-day machines, the Mach IV does a poorish job in protecting the rider from road water, but at least in this instance there seems to be a legitimate excuse. The makers claim that the front guard was wind-tunnel developed so that it would help to deliver a stream of cooling air to the middle cylinder.

For the American market, the Mach IV wears nothing but its pressed-steel rump. Fortunately, the European version comes with a quite effective stainless-steel rear mudguard. It tends to collect an oily residue from the triple exhausts, but can be wiped clean very easily.

In over 1,200 miles of running, the engine unit suffered no oil leaks.

The Mach IV is a machine of strong character and very considerable charm. The American reputation of unbridled, brute power gives a rather one-sided view. Certainly the power is there should you want to use it. But the Kawasaki also has a very aimiable side to its nature, and is equally content to amble along on a minimal throttle opening in a high gear.

Indeed, its slogging abilities – which are nowhere stressed in the makers' advertising – are particularly impressive. It would, for instance, take Hopton Bank (the long, 1-in-12 drag up to the Clee Hills, from the Cleobury Mortimer side) in top gear all the way.

Normally, of course, it would be better to drop down to fourth or third and that would be no hardship, for the Mach IV has a sweet gearbox, and with close positioning of the top three ratios, keeping the big blue beauty on song is easy.

Heavy fuel consumption? Well it is not really necessary to squirt the bike from point to point every time, although to do so is great fun – and worth the cost of the fuel!

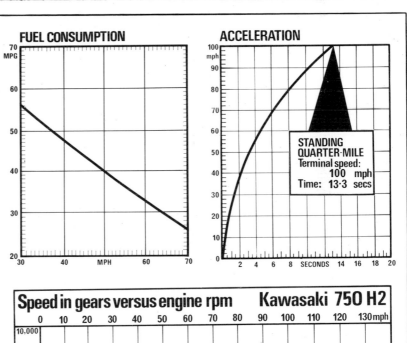

FUEL CONSUMPTION

ACCELERATION

STANDING QUARTER-MILE
Terminal speed:
100 mph
Time: 13·3 secs

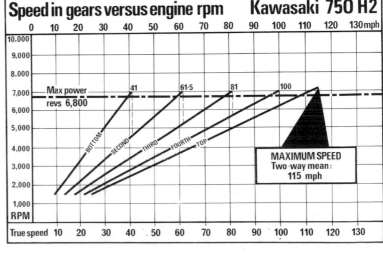

Speed in gears versus engine rpm   Kawasaki 750 H2

Max power revs 6,800

41   61·5   81   100

BOTTOM   SECOND   THIRD   FOURTH   TOP

MAXIMUM SPEED
Two-way mean:
115 mph

Kawasaki Z1000

There is one sure way to get respect from other road users when you are on two wheels. Ride a Kawasaki Z1000 four. The sheer majesty of the machine is enough to impress even lorry drivers. You glide along feeling like the king of the road, your lowly subjects clearing a swath through the traffic for your passing. The big Kawasaki has become a legend in its own lifetime.

That legend has been based on arm-wrenching performance. If you are the sort of person who gets kicks from taking off like a Bobcat from a carrier then no other machine will satisfy like the Z1000. That is a hallmark of the bike, and everybody on the road knows it. There is an almost erotic pleasure to be enjoyed in squirting the Kawa past a line of cars, feeling that you have been shot from a monster cannon.

The action is instantaneous on the big 1,015 cc four. Regardless of revs, a flick of the wrist on the twistgrip is enough to twang your arms taut and literally take your breath away.

The Z1000 surprisingly lacks the absolute top speed of its first 903 cc predecessors, but makes up for this in smoothness and docility. The first Z1 models were capable of a genuine 130 mph, but by comparison to the Z1000 were harsh, hairy and developed phenominal top end power – just as a double overhead camshaft should.

Despite higher gearing provided by a 33 tooth

rear sprocket instead of a 35 tooth one and an increase in bore size from 66 mm to 70 mm, the absolute top speed of the Z1000 with the rider flat on the tank is just under 125 mph – barely more than the 750 cc Honda and Suzuki fours – with the engine turning over at a leisurely 7,600 rpm. That is 400 revs short of the maximum 8,000 rpm, where the whistling all-roller bearing engine develops a claimed 83 bhp.

Why the Z1000 should be slower with over 1,000 cc more than the old nine hundred is a puzzle. But it should be no surprise that the bigger bike has less poke when the carburettor size has been dropped from 28 mm to 26 mm and the engine is pulling gearing that gives theoretical speeds of 130 mph and 147 mph in fourth and top at the red line of 8,000 rpm.

For all but the budding drag racers among us, that top end power will not be missed, for the Z1000 more than makes up for it in flexibility and gentlemanly manners. There is no doubt at all that the latest model is light years ahead for its smoothness, quietness and ease of operation.

In fact, the Z1000 is one of the few bikes – perhaps the only bike – on the market that offers a blend of outright performance on a par with the Italian Laverda 1000 with an equal measure of round-town unfussiness and simplicity of handling.

One end of the Z1000 performance spectrum is acceleration that rockets you from rest to 60 mph in a shade over 4 seconds and 100 mph in 11 seconds. At that speed the bike is still pulling hard enough for the rider to have to hang on hard. The other end of the spectrum is flexibility that allows the rider to trickle along in top gear at 16 mph and pull away smoothly without a jerk.

Clean carburation and a wide spread of torque give the Z1000 a light thirst for fuel. On low octane fuel, the bike eaked out 47 miles from each gallon. Including reserve, the fuel capacity is 3·6 gallons, much less than the big tank suggests.

High speed handling has been tremendously improved over the 900 four. At lower speeds – below 50 mph – it is much as before; light and easy and with a neutrality in the steering that belies the 560 lb tanked up weight of the machine. The broad spread of the handlebar helps, indeed it enhances the majestic feel of the bike, but coupled with wind pressure it also makes riding a strain at anything over 60 mph. Switching to a lower handlebar is made trickier than normal as the wiring runs through the tubing.

The steering geometry, a steep rake of 64 degrees and short trail of just $3\frac{1}{2}$ in, inevitably means that some degree of stability has to be sacrificed at very high speeds. And most riders agree that the Kawasaki lacks the sure-footedness of its Italian 1,000 cc equivalents.

Nevertheless, a measure of improvement in the Z1000 handling over the Z1 and Z900 has been achieved by more generous gusseting and stiffer suspension and should put the shine back on the big Kawasaki's tarnished reputation for wobbly

The twin disc brakes on the front wheel of the Kawasaki Z1000 are frighteningly ineffective in heavy rain

roadholding. Whether it is the light steering, squirmy tyres, light suspension damping, the frame or a mixture of all four, the Kawasaki will start to shake when cranked over on smooth surfaces at 90 mph – and that is an improvement. Its predecessors used to do it at speeds well below that.

With only one silencer either side, cornering clearance is even more generous and the first piece of hardwear to grind the tarmac is the prop stand. The stiffer suspension and needle-roller swing-arm pivots have helped here too, limiting the amount of squat during cornering (but that is

Specification

Engine: 1,015 cc (70 × 66 mm) double-overhead camshaft, transverse, in-line four. Six roller main bearings; needle-roller big ends. Wet sump lubrication with gear pump and paper-element oil filter. Compression ratio, 8·7 to 1. Four 26-mm choke Mikuni carburettors with lever-operated cold-start jets; paper-element air filter. Claimed maximum power, 83 bhp at 8,000 rpm. Maximum torque, 58·5 lb-ft at 6,500 rpm.

Transmission: Primary drive by spur gears. Wet, multiplate clutch and five-speed gearbox. Overall ratios: 12·1, 8·3, 6·35, 5·26 and 4·64 to 1. Final drive by endless, sealed EK630S 0·5 × 0·375-in roller chain.

Electrical Equipment: Twin coil ignition. 12-volt, 14-amp-hour battery and thyristor voltage control. Semi-sealed beam 7-in diameter headlamp with 45/40-watt main filament. Direction indicators; starter motor; three fuses.

Brakes: Hydraulically-operated 11·6-in diameter duplex disc front, single disc rear. Floating front calipers, double-acting rear.

Tyres: Dunlop Gold Seal, 3·25H 19 ribbed F6 front, 4·00H18 patterned K87 rear. Laced spoke-type, steel-rim wheels.

Suspension: Telescopic front fork. Pivoted rear fork with five-position spring preload adjustment.

Frame: All-welded duplex tube cradle.

Dimensions: Wheelbase, 59·25 in; seat height, 32·5 in; ground clearance, 7 in; handlebar width, 32·25 in; castor angle, 64°; trail, 3·5 in; turning circle, 16 ft; all unladen.

Weight: 550 lb including one gallon of fuel.

Fuel Capacity: 3·6 UK gal (4·3 US gal) including 7 pt reserve.

Sump Oil Capacity: 6·5 pt.

Manufacturer: Kawasaki Heavy Industries Ltd, (Motorcycle Division), World Trade Centre, Tokyo.

Performance

Maximum Speeds (Mean): 124·4 mph; 113 mph with rider sitting normally.
Best One-way Speed: 131 mph – dry track, strong tail wind.
Braking Distance – from 30 mph: 27 ft.
Fuel Consumption: 43 miles/UK gal (35·7 miles/US gal).
Oil Consumption: 1,000 mpp.
Minimum Non-snatch Speed: 16 mph in top gear.
Speedo Accuracy:

Indicated mph	30	40	50	60	70
Actual mph	26·9	36·4	45·9	54·8	63·8

about as far as the bonuses go).

The rear springs have been changed to dual-rate 123/174 lb/in boneshakers while the front fork contains 45 pounders that give an adequate ride but do not take kindly to bumpy surfaces, responding with a clattery and uncontrolled amount of bouncing once a few miles have been covered.

The addition of an extra brake disc at the front together with a rear brake disc may have upset the suspension with the higher unsprung weight, but they certainly do bolster the braking power. The two front units with floating calipers are capable of locking the front wheel at will in the dry with a pleasant degree of sensitivity. Likewise the same size – 11·6-in diameter – rear disc offers progressive stopping.

But like similarly equipped bikes with three stainless-steel discs, under certain conditions, in the wet the brakes are completely ineffective. Invariably when rain was heavy, the bike was not being ridden fast enough to fling off water, and the discs were cold, you would find yourself sailing up to a stop light with no more than a prayer to pull you up.

The sooner the Transport and Road Research Laboratory work on this subject is completed and acted upon, the better.

In other departments, the Z1000 is 'standard Japanese'. The five-speed gearbox has a light action spoiled only by clunkiness when notching bottom from neutral. Neutral is easy to find at rest because the mechanism is designed to prevent a rider passing through neutral into second at a stop. That is still a unique feature. The controls are all very light, including the throttle and clutch lever. Incidentally, the clutch

The Z1000 engine is one of the toughest power units in motor cycling; it develops 83 bhp at 8,000 rpm and there is hardly any need for fine tuning to keep it delivering awe-inspiring performance

survived several full-blooded drag starts with only slight swelling.

The Z1000 is a big bike though. The cosy seat is not unduly high at 32½ in but being broader than most will cause anyone with less than a 32-in inside leg to be searching for the ground with their toes.

Although the higher gearing lessens vibration from the engine, the high-frequency buzz is still there, particularly above 5,000 rpm. Its not great trouble to the rider but the well-spread mirrors deteriorate into a blur above 75 mph in top.

Lighting is adequate, although many riders will want to uprate the headlamp if they want power to match the bike's performance. Starting on the button was always achieved but there is an indication that the start jet metering was over-generous as the engine started hunting almost as soon as it was running.

Chain rear drive on such a potent bike such as the Z1000 may seem an anachronism in these days of increasing use of shaft drive. but Kawasaki appear to have overcome many of the drawbacks with their Enuma ¾-in pitch chain. Each link has its lubricant sealed in by O-rings and the fact that the chain remained properly tensioned over 500 miles of general use is ample testimony to its effectiveness. The price the rider pays for such heavy chain is that it vibrates as it clatters around the 15-tooth gearbox sprocket when opening up from low speeds in a high gear.

But that is a small point when measured against the host of detail changes that have contributed to the metamorphosis of the Z900 into the Z1000.

On a pound per performance basis the Kawasaki Z1000 remains the King.

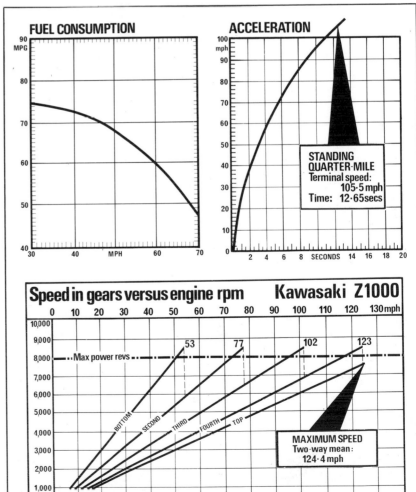

FUEL CONSUMPTION

ACCELERATION

STANDING
QUARTER-MILE
Terminal speed:
105·5 mph
Time: 12·65 secs

Speed in gears versus engine rpm   **Kawasaki Z1000**

Max power revs

53   77   102   123

BOTTOM   SECOND   THIRD   FOURTH   TOP

MAXIMUM SPEED
Two-way mean:
124·4 mph

Laverda 750SF

To students of modern motor cycle design, there is very little in the specification of the Laverda 750SF twin to get excited about. By contemporary standards, the machine is positively archaic and should have been pensioned off years ago.

Its engine is a 744 cc parallel twin with a single-overhead camshaft and drive to the rear wheel is by a triplex primary chain, five-speed gearbox and a simple rear chain. The bike is heavy and until a rider is familiar with it, apparently very awkward to ride.

On the other hand, such an analysis ignores many of the reasons for the existence of superbikes. For the Laverda 750SF is one of the most aggressively attractive motor cycles to appear from Italy and to many eyes still puts the bigger 981 cc three-cylinder Laverda into the shade on looks alone.

The engine, originally conceived in the late 1960s as a 650 cc unit, was unashamedly based on the very popular 250 cc Honda CB72 twin with sharply-angled cylinder finning running to the

top of the cambox. The whole line of the machine suggests speed – the tank is long and classically-styled and the rear seat can be an optional racing-style unit with a sleek back, while by very subtle positioning of the handlebars, footrests and running gear, the whole picture is of a machine made for fast and aggressive riding.

The 750SF did not always look that way. As originally designed it looked strangely cumbersome and it was not until 1972 that it gained the looks that have kept it a favourite despite the many more exotic machines that have come onto the market in the meantime.

In appearance, the latest versions of the SF are well up to date, with cast-alloy five-spoke wheels and potent disc brakes, two on the front wheel and one on the back. Laverda were the first to adopt the excellent Nippon Seikki instruments from Japan in favour of the poor Italian examples and still use them, the current versions being identical to those found on the bigger Hondas. Switchgear is also from Japan and is the same as that found on Suzukis.

The performance of the SF however, shows the limits of the engine. Once one of the fastest and most powerful 750 cc machines, the SF is now merely average with a top speed of 118 mph and a standing quarter-mile time of 13·8 sec, figures that can be equalled or bettered by the quicker 550 cc machines. But the 750SF has many other virtues which were shown up when testing the 1975 model (identical to the latest example except for the wheels and brakes). New in 1975 were the twin front discs, replacing a massive four-leading-shoe drum brake, and a more powerful German Bosch quartz-halogen headlamp. A year earlier, bigger Delorto carburettors with 32-mm chokes and accelerator pumps plus a higher lift camshaft, had given the 750SF a sportier nature.

While much more lively in the upper rev ranges, the bike is still flexible enough to pull well at low revs. Most of the power is developed between 5,000 and 8,000 rpm, the rev limit, with a maximum of 65 bhp. The bike is just as happy to chuff along at a walking pace in bottom gear while idling at 1,000 rpm.

Despite the use of the accelerator pump carbs, fuel consumption has improved on the Laverda SF over the years, and the latest version benefits from leaner mixture settings. Overall the 750SF returned between 42 and 48 mpg, offering a total range of 180 miles. A drawback of the leaner carburation proved to be a reluctance to accept full throttle during acceleration tests, and which necessitated heavy slipping of the clutch instead of the usually more effective, and quicker getaways offered by spinning the rear wheel.

One of the most stylish 750 cc machines ever made, the Laverda 750SF could be fitted with either a dual seat (far left) or the more attractive racing-pattern single seat (below)

The 750SF is a picture of ruggedness, which in reality is not far off the truth. The engine is built to massive proportions with a four-roller-bearing crankshaft having wide big ends and running in thick castings. Bore and stroke are slightly oversquare at 80 mm by 74 mm and the chain-driven overhead camshaft runs in big roller bearings. Unusually on a modern bike the electrical system is supplied by a dynamo which is rubber vee-belt driven from the offside end of the crankshaft, as is the electric starter.

The first acquaintance with the bike is hardly impressive either, particularly if you have to ride

substantial and produces rewards both in longevity and giving a feeling of being glued to the road. With a weight of over 500 lb it is a credit to Laverda that the 750SF performs as it does.

Set up for fast road work and most comfortable when breezing along at a 90 mph gait, the drape-over-the-tank rider's stance makes slow riding a chore. The footrests are adjustable, as on the 981 cc three, giving a fair range and making up for the tall seat height. Two seats are available, the racing type with a toolbox in the rear, giving just about enough room for two or a more mundane-looking dual seat.

With the aid of perfectly-matched suspension, the bike sails securely through corners without deviating from its path. Spring rates are hard but to be expected on this sort of machine.

The tyres spoil the handling when the machine is cranked near the limit. Metzelers may be fine on a BMW but they are hardly suited to the Laverda. Dunlop TT100s as were fitted to earlier SFs and, we are told, are now the standard equipment, give much better grip on the sidewalls.

Although the engine is passably quite mechanically, the triplex-chain primary drive produced some chatter under power and the clutch, while normally smooth and quiet, replied to the

---

Specification

Engine: 744 cc (80 × 74 mm) overhead-camshaft, parallel twin. Light-alloy cylinder block and head. Two ball and two roller main bearings; roller bearing outboard of engine sprocket; double-row caged-roller big ends. Wet sump lubrication. Compression ratio, 8·9 to 1. Two 36-mm Delorto carburettors; accelerator pumps; handlebar-operated cold start jets; paper-element air filter. Claimed maximum power, 65 bhp at 7,000 rpm.
Transmission: Triplex primary chain. Wet, multiplate inboard clutch. Five-speed gearbox. Overall ratios: 12·1, 8·7, 6·35, 5·42 and 4·62 to 1. Final chain, 0·625 × 0·375 in. Mph at 1,800 rpm in top gear, 30.
Electrical Equipment: Coil ignition. 12-volt, 24-amp-hour battery. 150-watt dynamo. 6·5-in diameter headlamp; 60/65-watt quartz-halogen main bulb. Starter motor; direction indicators; headlamp flasher; dual air horns.
Brakes: Double-disc 11-in diameter front; double leading shoe, 9-in diameter drum rear.
Tyres: Metzeler, 3·50 × 18-in ribbed front; 4·00 × 18-in C6 studded rear.
Suspension: Ceriana front fork. Pivoted rear fork with three-position spring preload adjustment.
Frame: Duplex loop spine type.
Dimensions: Wheelbase, 57·5 in; seat height, 31·5 in; ground clearance, 8·5 in; all unladen.
Weight: 500 lb including approximately one gallon of fuel.
Fuel Capacity: 4·25 UK gal (5·1 US gal) including 5 pt reserve.
Sump Oil Capacity: 5·5 pt.
Manufacturer: Moto Laverda SpA, 36042 Breganze, Italy.

Performance
Maximum Speed (Mean): 117·5 mph with rider wearing racing leathers.
Best One-way Speed: 118 mph – dry track, light cross wind.
Braking Distance – from 30 mph: 27 ft.
Fuel Consumption: 58 miles/UK gal (48·1 miles/US gal) at 60 mph.
Minimum Non-snatch Speed: 19 mph.
Speedo Accuracy:

Indicated mph	30	40	50	60	70
Actual mph	28·2	37·4	46·6	56·6	65·7

The age of the Laverda's design is indicated by the use of a belt-driven dynamo on the front of the engine
Top right: brakes are stunningly powerful Brembo twin disc units

it in town. Out of its element on the fast and open road, the 750SF feels rough and gawky, and only really comes alive when driven hard and rushed through demanding bends. Then the message come through loud and clear, that it is a true sporting bike in the best tradition.

At speeds below 25 mph the steering is heavy and there is some degree of 'understeer' that requires an application of pressure to the handlebar to maintain a line. But buzzing the engine to 7,500 rpm through the gearbox (with almost BMW-like clunks with ragged changes, or crisp ones clutchless), exhaust booming out its deep note, the 750SF smooths out well for a vertical twin, and the steering becomes progressively more taut, just like a racing bike.

A reason for the smoothness compared to other vertical twins is the total mass of engine and the spine-type frame, made of thick wall tubing and gusseting.

By common standards the frame is very

standing start tests by grating on the take up and subsequently slipping at speed.

Augmenting the handling well, the brakes are fabulous, despite the all-up weight of the Laverda. Drawback is that the dual discs increase the unsprung weight over the old drum unit.

Electrically, the bike was faultless, but we were surprised that Laverda have retained the small and archaic CEV rear lamp while replacing the headlamp with the brilliant Bosch quartz-halogen unit. No praise can be great enough for the fabulous air horns. Instruments and switchgear are good in quality and convenience.

Varied and well finished, the toolkit is easily found by unscrewing one of the sidepanels, and proved sufficient for most of the usual tasks.

Apart from poorly completed chromework – nickel was showing through on the silencers – the general finish of the bike is good. The only real snags we feel were a neutral lamp that flickered on regardlessly towards the end of the test, and buckled rear wheel adjuster, legacy of an attempt to break traction in the acceleration tests.

If you are turned on by the Italian looks and aura and want a solid and reliable machine – a man's bike as they would have said once – then the SF is the only machine for you.

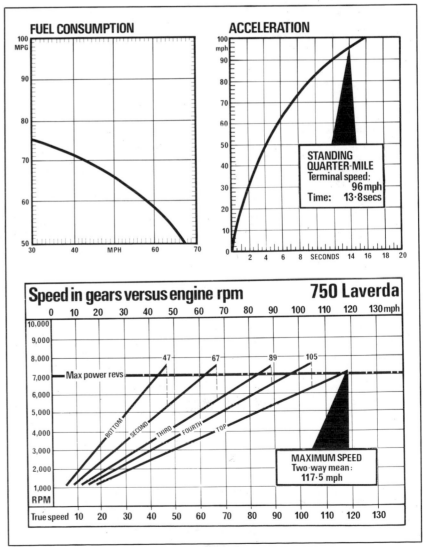

FUEL CONSUMPTION

ACCELERATION

STANDING QUARTER-MILE
Terminal speed: 96 mph
Time: 13·8 secs

Speed in gears versus engine rpm — 750 Laverda

Max power revs

47 67 89 105

BOTTOM SECOND THIRD FOURTH TOP

MAXIMUM SPEED
Two-way mean: 117·5 mph

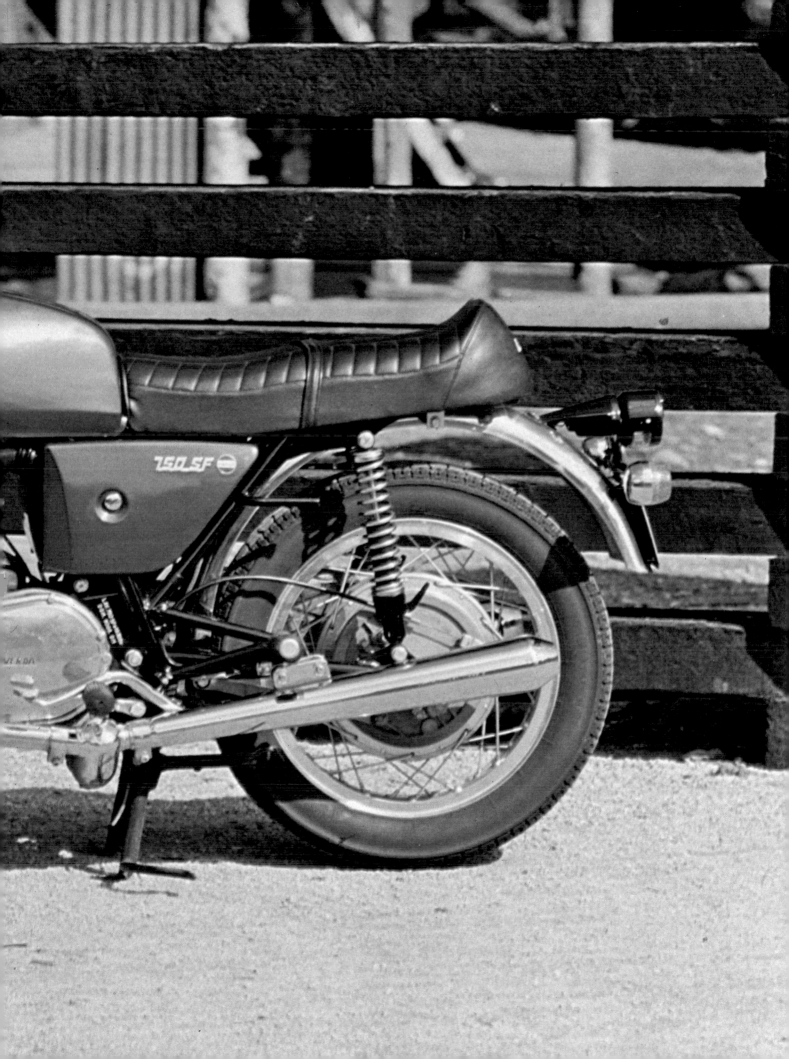

Laverda Jota 1000

Thundering performance is fashionable again, and bikes that can top 135 mph are almost commonplace. But in the mid-1970s the atmosphere was very different. The Middle East oil embargoes had many effects, and one of them was to defuse the power of many of the superbikes. Few had the potential to squeeze past 125 mph and manufacturers had turned to making their products quiet, smooth and comfortable.

An exception was Laverda. Their British importer, Roger Slater, had been campaigning one of their 981 cc three-cylinder models in production racing with great success, and he wanted Laverda to be acclaimed as the fastest machine on sale. The little Italian factory had been making a number of specially tuned models for the British market, the 3CE, and this had proved to be the fastest motor cycle ever tested by *Motor Cycle* at a mean 133·3 mph at MIRA. For continued supremacy in stock racing, particularly the Avon Roadrunner series, some-

thing more potent was necessary, however.

So the Jota was introduced. Like the 3CE, it had a three-cylinder double-overhead camshaft engine, with a novel crank arrangement with the middle piston at top dead centre when the outers were at bottom dead centre, a layout that accentuated the bark of the exhaust even further.

New were five-spoke cast-alloy wheels, disc brakes on both wheels and a neat folding seat with a streamlined tail section. But there were no pretentions to home comforts. The Jota is still a brutal motor cycle, and although it has a larger capacity stablemate in the form of the 1200, it is still one of the fastest you can buy.

The engine is massively powerful and feels it. The unit jangles and rumbles and like a racing engine has a sharply defined power band. When it hits the band the exhaust crackles and the bike catapults the rider forward breathtakingly. Not for nothing are the handlebars adjustable into a racing position – you need it to stay on.

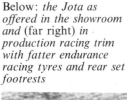

Below: *the Jota as offered in the showroom and* (far right) *in production racing trim with fatter endurance racing tyres and rear set footrests*

At the test track the Jota (Italian for a quick dance for three, so they say) proved its supremacy by topping the 3CE by over 4 mph. Its mean two-way top speed was 137·8 mph – miles faster than anything else then currently available and it was the first over-the-counter production roadster to better 140 mph in one direction with a figure of 140·04 mph.

In racing the Jota was fully justified after winning the Avon series in the hands of Peter Davies in 1976.

For racing some degree of compromise is necessary so there are a number of options available. The air filter can be dispensed with, as we did, the exhaust system offers less resistance than normal (to the level of being illegal in many European countries) and the gearbox can have very close ratios (which were fitted to the test bike, the one raced by Davies). A change in the layshaft return gear closes up the gaps between the gears. Bottom gear, at 9·5 to 1, is 18 percent higher than the standard ratio.

With or without the options, the Jota makes a fabulous machine. On the road, steering and roadholding are both beyond reproach while the braking is simply eye-popping. The engine has a lazy sounding note that makes the acceleration extremely deceptive. Open up the three Delorto carbs and the rest of the world seems to go into reverse.

With the close-ratio gearbox and highest gearing the speeds at maximum revs in each cog read like science fiction. Normally, the Laverda 3C revs to 7,500 rpm, as marked on the Japanese-made Nippon Denso rev counter, but the Jota can be revved safely to 8,500, though 8,000 is more than enough. At eight, the high bottom gear goes on forever, peaking out at 64 mph, second takes you on to 88 mph, third whistles past the ton to 111 mph, fourth is good enough to beat any 1976 machine in top at 130 mph and top gear peaks at 141 mph.

Not surprisingly, riding the Jota in town is made more awkward as the practical minimum speed in bottom gear is a shade over 10 mph, and some clutch slipping is needed when pulling away quickly from rest.

This showed up convincingly during the standing quarter mile tests. It was impossible to use full power when slipping the clutch for fear of frying the plates and the sticky Dunlop endurance tyre fitted prevented spinning the rear wheel. So the first few yards of the quarter-mile were taken gingerly and chopped vital seconds from the elapsed time.

Despite this, the Jota thundered down the strip to record a mean time of 13·05 sec with a terminal speed of 110·55 mph. Geared for the quarter, there is no doubt that the bike would have clocked very low twelves at around 113 mph.

Either way, the Jota can blow off anything on the road.

What is remarkable about the Jota is that this performance is achieved without sacrificing too many of the manners expected of a roadster. The bike produces a magnificent sound – winding open the throttle at low revs releases a sharp bark from the three-into-two exhaust system that mellows into a crisp wail on full power. But the engine runs happily on four-star fuel despite the 10 to 1 compression ratio and, being so big, has adequate torque for quick getaways in almost any circumstances.

All the same, there is always the animal in the bike lurking in the depths of its massive crankcase. It whirrs and whines, particularly the triplex primary chain and never really likes being run at less than a fast lick.

The reason lies in the power characteristics. The double-overhead-camshaft head contains racing cams which are only happy in opening the bucket-follower operated valves at over 5,000 rpm, preferably with the aid of a megaphone exhaust. This gives 90 bhp at 7,600 rpm.

The effect is most distinctive in top gear. Below 70 mph the engine baulks at full throttle. But at 90 it becomes interested, at the ton it is on the boil and beyond that the bike feels like it will keep accelerating for ever.

Specification

Engine: 981 cc (75 × 74 mm) double-overhead camshaft, transverse, in-line three. Light-alloy cylinder block and head. Four caged-roller main bearings with needle roller outrigger on drive side; caged-roller big ends. Wet sump lubrication with gear pump and oil cooler. Compression ratio, 10 to 1. Three 32-mm choke Delorto carburettors with lever-operated cold-start jets; optional paper element air filter. Maximum claimed power, 90 bhp at 7,600 rpm.

Transmission: Triplex primary chain with slipper tensioner. Wet, multiplate clutch and five-speed gearbox. Overall ratios: 9·51, 6·90, 5·45, 4·65 and 4·29 to 1. Final drive by 0·625 × 0·375-in chain with vane type shock absorber in rear-wheel hub. Mph at 1,000 rpm in top gear, 17·7.

Electrical Equipment: Bosch electronic flywheel-magneto ignition with external coils. 12-volt, 27-amp-hour battery and 125-watt alternator. 7·5-in diameter headlamp with 60/55-watt halogen main bulb. Starter motor and four fuses.

Brakes: Hydraulically-operated Brembo 11-in (279-mm) diameter double disc front, single rear with double-acting calipers.

Tyres: Dunlop TT100, 4·10 × S18-in front, 4·25 × S18-in rear. Cast light-alloy wheels.

Suspension: Ceriani telescopic front fork. Pivoted rear fork with Ceriani spring damper units and three-position spring preload adjustment.

Frame: Welded duplex cradle with 2·5-in diameter spine.

Dimensions: Wheelbase, 58·5 in; ground clearance, 5·5 in; seat height, 32·5 in; castor angle 63°; trail, 5·5 in; turning circle 16 ft; all unladen.

Weight: 522 lb including approximately one gallon of fuel.

Fuel Capacity: 4·25 UK gal (5·1 US gal) including 3 pt reserve.

Sump Oil Capacity: 5·5 pt.

Manufacturer: Moto Laverda SpA, 36042 Breganze, Italy.

Performance

Maximum Speeds (Mean): 137·8 mph; 125·95 mph with rider in two-piece outfit sitting normally.

Best One-way Speed: 140·04 mph – dry track, slight tail wind.

Braking Distance – from 30 mph: 25 ft 5 in.

Fuel Consumption: 42·6 miles/UK gal (35·4 miles/US gal) overall.

Oil Consumption: approximately 500 mpp overall.

Minimum Non-snatch Speed: 24 mph in top gear.

Speedo Accuracy:

Indicated mph	30	40	50	60	70	80	90
Actual mph	28·9	38·4	47·9	58·9	69·9	80·9	91·9

Nevertheless, it can still run economically, returning 42·5 mpg, giving well over 150 miles range on the 4 gallon tank.

As well as offering stunning performance, Laverda make the Jota more appealing by not losing sight of the need for a quality of finish and detailing that puts other Italian bikes to shame.

On the Jota there is a cosy seat that hinges up and is lockable, superb instruments which are also very accurate and – something of a rarity on any bike – fully adjustable hand and foot controls.

The handlebar can be raised from a full racing position to a normal touring stance in minutes with socket key while the footrests can be rotated, giving almost 3 inches of adjustment. Variable length gear levers are also available. The upshot is that although the seat is fairly high at 32 inches, the slim profile of the bike can accommodate a broad variety of rider statures.

The controls blend beautifully to the rider's hands. Both levers are contoured and the fingers slide over them naturally. The switches, identical almost to those found on Suzukis, are substantial, neat and very easy to use.

Apart from a heavy clutch action and a gear change which could occasionally be noisy in the lower gears, the controls generally set a very high standard. So the rider is in a good position to sample the Laverda's excellent handling to the full.

The steering, which has unusual geometry resulting from fork legs which are parallel to the steering stem, is natural at all speeds and the bike can be cranked over without need for correction at the handlebar to hold a line.

Only criticism is a slight jumpiness in the steering that occurs above 90 mph which is cured, as when the bike is raced by Slater, by using the racing yokes from the 750 SFC production racer, bringing the forks parallel to the stem.

The cornering clearance is immense, too, despite the large generator cover, and in road use the rider need have no fear of touching anything. Even so, Roger Slater feels he has to stiffen up the suspension which, in day-to-day circumstances, is a perfect compromise between ride

and road holding but which squats too much under the immense cornering loads offered by the Dunlop tyres and limits clearance on the right.

Compared with the 3CE, a larger section 4·25-in rear tyre is used on the Jota, which is made more secure by using a negative angle on the face of the cast light-alloy wheel to hold the tyre bead against the side walls of the rim. The idea is to get better traction at the back end, but if you are like Peter Davies and prefer a little more, fit the Dunlop Endurance KR91 tyres as were used at the Hutchinson 100 races when Peter came second and were still fitted when we tested the bike at MIRA. The grip with these is massive but, nevertheless, they still had shortcomings. Powering out of the 90 mph bends on the MIRA No. 2 circuit resulted in some wiggles at the back end, but you had to be right on the limit to provoke it.

With three 11-in discs, the braking was as good as can be on a machine weighing 504 lb. The tyres helped particularly to give a 30 mph stopping distance of 25 ft.

A chain drive the Jota may have, but it is engineered for the minimum of problems by correct geometry relative to the swinging arm pivot (incidentally now on needle bearings) and chain wear is very low.

Everything else is just as one should expect of a machine of its price bracket. Lighting from the 60-watt halogen headlamp is more than adequate for the bike's speed, the tools are generous and strong while the finish is 100 per cent.

The electric starting may be noisy but it is reliable. Further impressive features are the easy-to-use main stand, fuss-free electronic ignition and a pair of horns that would wake the dead (let alone car drivers!). Altogether, the barrel-chested Jota is a rider's bike, the sort of machine that responds best to skilful and attentive riding,

Handlebars on Laverdas are fully adjustable

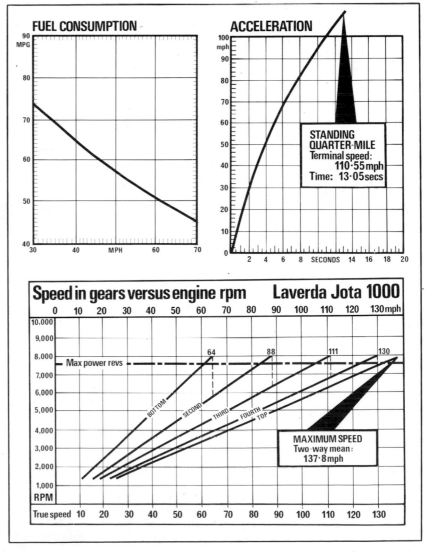

FUEL CONSUMPTION

ACCELERATION

STANDING QUARTER-MILE
Terminal speed: 110·55 mph
Time: 13·05 secs

Speed in gears versus engine rpm   Laverda Jota 1000

Max power revs

64   88   111   130

BOTTOM   SECOND   THIRD   FOURTH   TOP

MAXIMUM SPEED
Two-way mean: 137·8 mph

True speed 10 20 30 40 50 60 70 80 90 100 110 120 130

Moto Guzzi Le Mans 850

No Compromise! That clarion call would probably be denied by many of the Italian factories like Moto Guzzi, but it is obvious from their undiluted sporting machines that they will go to any lengths to satisfy that aim.

The 844 cc Le Mans is a classic case. Offered by Moto Guzzi as the top of the range sportster in 1976 it was neither fast for its size or particularly quick over the quarter mile compared to many other outwardly less potent machines. But where it counts, on the open road or on the race tracks, the mighty Le Mans has few peers. It is both fast and agile and responds well to tuning, as has been borne out by the marque's overwhelming success in production machine racing.

Like Ducati, Moto Guzzi have paid close attention to the basic credentials of the machine.

Basic hardwear for the production road racer or the high-speed cruiser alike; the 850 cc Moto Guzzi Le Mans vee-twin

As the name of the bike suggests it is closely associated with racing. Le Mans is the home of the 24-hour Bol d'Or endurance race and while not having the same level of success as Ducati in this type of competition, Moto Guzzi learned the same lessons: that a slim and light motor cycle with a very stiff frame can afford to give away disproportionate amounts of horsepower to more unweildy but potent racers.

It is ironic that the engine of the Le Mans was never originally intended for a motor cycle. Developed as a lightweight power unit for a military cross country vehicle it did however have obvious potential for a two-wheeler. Being a 90-degree vee-twin it has the inherent smoothness and rhythm that has always been appealing to motor cyclists.

The first engines, with a 700 cc capacity, were put into touring bikes, placed across the frame so that it was natural that the transmission should have shaft drive. This has remained on the Le Mans, proving a boon in long-distance racing.

The engine is ideal for a motor cycle for one basic reason. Not only is it smooth, but its narrow crankcase means that it can be set low down in the frame for light handling and still give a large degree of ground clearance.

The unit is extremely robustly built. External ribbing on the cases and a massive forged single-throw crankshaft are further strengthened by generous plain main and big-end bearings. There are many similarities to the BMW, but a very significant difference is that the camshaft is above the crankshaft, in the crotch of the vee with short pushrods and rockers opening the valves. With lighter valve gear, the Guzzi is far less sensitive to over-revving than the BMW.

Bore and stroke are slightly oversquare, at 83 mm by 78 mm, and the barrels are interesting for their chrome plated bores which are unique on a four-stroke motor cycle.

And as befits a sports machine, the level of tune is comparable to the early works endurance racers. Compression ratio is a hefty 10·2 to 1 and the engine breaths through two 36-mm choke Delorto carburettors with no more filtering than a couple of velocity stacks and stone guards.

Yet apart from a level of bustling noise that is not totally out of place on the bike, there is an initial indication of the Le Mans' civility. It starts up from cold promptly after using the starting jet lever and punching the electric starter button on

the right-hand clip-on handlebar. And it runs cleanly on four-star fuel despite the high compression ratio – this hints at good combustion chamber design. The feeling of utter civility ends when you open up the Le Mans. The loud gasping from the intakes indicates that the bike wants to go fast. Unlike the touring 850-T3 model, the Le Mans develops comparatively little torque at low revs and wills the rider to go faster and faster.

The bike has a pleasant long-legged feel too that makes it deceptively fast despite the over-optimism of the speedometer.

Specification

Engine: 844 cc (83 × 78 mm) overhead valve, transverse, 90° vee-twin. Light-alloy heads and barrels; chrome-plated bores. Two plain main bearings; plain big ends. Wet sump lubrication; gear pump. Compression ratio, 10·2 to 1. Two Delorto PHF 36-mm choke carburettors with accelerator pumps; cable-operated cold-start jets. Claimed maximum power, 80 bhp at 7,300 rpm.
Transmission: Two-plate dry clutch on crankshaft to primary spur gears (ratio 21/17). Five-speed gearbox. Overall ratios: 11·64, 8·08, 6·1, 5·06 and 4·37 to 1. Final drive by shaft and spiral-bevel gears (ratio 33/7). Mph at 1,000 rpm in top gear, 16·7.
Electrical Equipment: Coil ignition. 12-volt, 32-amp-hour battery and 280-watt alternator. 7-in diameter headlamp with 45/40-watt main bulb. Four fuses with spares. Starter motor.
Brakes: Brembo hydraulically-operated 11·75-in diameter perforated cast-iron double disc front, 9·5-in diameter rear. Front left and rear controlled by foot pedal with load limiting on rear.
Tyres: Metzeler, 3·25 × V18-in front ribbed. Avon Roadrunner, 4·10 × V18-in rear. Cast aluminium-alloy wheels.
Suspension: Moto Guzzi telescopic front fork. Pivoted rear fork with five-position spring preload adjustment.
Frame: Welded duplex tube cradle with removable bottom tubes.
Dimensions: Wheelbase, 59 in; ground clearance, 7·5 in; seat height, 29·5 in; handlebar width, 29 in; castor angle 61°; trail, 3·8 in; turning circle, 15 ft 3 in; all unladen.
Weight: 485 lb including approximately one gallon of fuel.
Fuel Capacity: 5 UK gal (6 US gal) including 5 pt reserve.
Sump Oil Capacity: 5 pt.
Manufacturer: Siemm Moto Guzzi SpA, Mandello del Lario, Como, Italy.

Performance

Maximum Speeds (Mean): 123·4 mph; 115 mph with rider sitting normally.
Best One-way Speed: 125·9 mph – dry track, 10 mph three-quarter tail wind.
Braking Distance – from 30 mph: 30 ft 4 in.
Fuel Consumption: 39·6 miles/UK gal (32·9 miles/US gal).
Oil Consumption: 375 mpp overall.
Minimum Non-snatch Speed: 16 mph in top gear.
Speedo Accuracy:

Indicated mph	30	40	50	60	70	80	90
Actual mph	21·6	30·4	39·2	47·8	56·4	66·5	76·6

High-speed cruising at an indicated 125 to 130 mph could be comfortably indulged in. The fact that this is a true speed of around 110 mph makes it no less impressive, particularly as the Le Mans is totally secure and smooth at this speed.

With the rider flat on the tank the mean top speed at MIRA was 123·4 mph at 7,500 rpm in top gear. With the engine developing a claimed 80 bhp at 7,300 rpm this suggests that the Le Mans is perfectly geared for its power output. The riding position is more of a racing crouch, with the clip-on handlebars and rear-mounted footrests urging the rider to keep out of the breeze behind the small fairing. Like this the Le Mans can still clock 115 mph, making it one of the fastest roadsters, even in 1978 when the quicker seven-fifties can top 125 mph flat out but are less flexible and unsuitable for continuous high-speed riding due to their sit-up-and-beg riding stances.

With a top gear ratio of 4·37 to 1 and the loping beat of the engine, the Le Mans pleasingly lacks the busy nature of the Japanese fours. But the overall high gearing, and the closeness of the five gearbox ratios, which are part of the reason for the bike's suitability for racing, spoil the standing quarter mile potential.

Figures of 14 sec and 98·9 mph are hardly impressive, equating only with touring bikes (indeed, this is only 0·1 sec slower than the 850-T3). A closer look at the acceleration graph shows that a full second is lost on the initial start, which with the additional 4 mph at the end of the run translates into a respectable figure.

Why this is so is not difficult to see. Bottom gear is fairly high and although the two-plate dry clutch is light in action it does not like taking up the drive on full blooded starts. The shaft drive also makes life difficult by extending the rear suspension and limiting the amount of wheel-spin possible.

By far the most impressive feature of the machine is its handling. Made of straight thick-walled tubing the frame is immensely strong and at high speed the bike has a degree of security that is uncanny. Like the feel of the engine, it has the effect of giving the impression that the machine is going much slower than it really is.

The suspension and front fork are well balanced, with optimum spring rates and damping, the only fault being the difficulty of altering the rear spring preload adjusters which are obscured by the close proximity of the silencers.

Like all in-line machines there is some torque reaction from the crankshaft when blipping the throttle or when changing gear quickly. It can also be embarrassing when you miss a gear, which is quite easy on the Le Mans because of the inordinate length of the lever and the need to change gear slowly to prevent clunks.

The steering is superb. Complimenting the high speed handling with tautness, the fork, with a 61 degree rake angle and 3·8 inches of trail, gives a totally different feel from a Ducati with a lightness at low speed that makes dense traffic a good deal less daunting.

The brakes are equally brilliant. Unique on a current two-wheeler the brakes offer feel and immense power arising from the use of the connected rear and front left discs. These are operated from the foot lever and for normal use nothing else is needed. But for real eye-popping stops the other hand lever-operated front disc can be called into action. Being nearly of 12-in diameter in perforated cast iron, the discs can lock the wheel at the will of the rider.

But for balanced use the rear disc is only 9 in and is more than good enough. The only limitation on braking is the quality and condition of the tyres.

The basic electrical gear on the Le Mans should be a model for other manufacturers too. A massive 280-watt alternator sits on the front of the crankshaft and feeds a monster 32-amp-hour battery. But the headlamp is a 45-watt unit that could usefully be replaced by a quartz-halogen unit, and the switchgear is the Mickey-Mouse-like barrel type first seen on Benellis that is neither reliable or easy to use.

So under the skin of the Le Mans is a motor cycle of indisputable quality. The surface lets it down, for the finish is very poor. The seat, a single moulding in foam rubber split soon after the bike was picked up; this was changed in design during late 1977 – it may be an improvement. The lining on the tank soon peeled after fuel was spilled on it and the matt of the exhaust pipes was soon tarnished.

This bike has plenty to offer the competitive sporting rider. If he is able to overlook the wrinkles then the road rider too should be rewarded by the basic integrity of the Guzzi Le Mans.

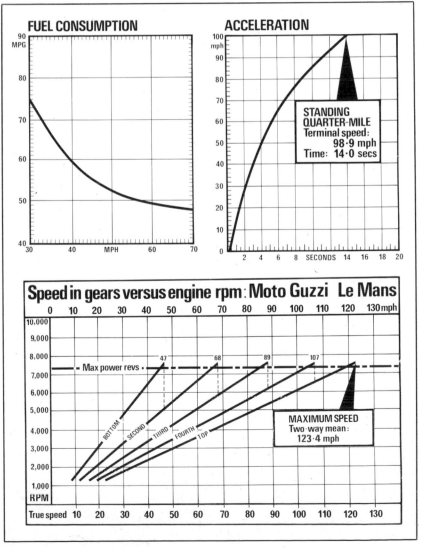

FUEL CONSUMPTION

ACCELERATION

STANDING QUARTER-MILE
Terminal speed: 98·9 mph
Time: 14·0 secs

Speed in gears versus engine rpm: Moto Guzzi Le Mans

Max power revs   47   68   89   107

BOTTOM   SECOND   THIRD   FOURTH   TOP

MAXIMUM SPEED
Two-way mean:
123·4 mph

MV Agusta 750S America

A motor cycle is more than a means of getting from A to B and can offer even more than the fun and freedom with which it is popularly associated. A motor cycle can be a passport to a fantasy existence. And the most convincing proof of this is the MV Agusta 750S America.

A dream in its red finish, set off by matt silver castings and gold alloy wheels, the 750S is more than a motor cycle. Riding one transports you into the fantasy worlds of the works racer and the millionaire – both at once. The mixture of a racing riding stance with low-mounted instruments and controls, the slim and sonorous four-cylinder engine and the roar of the exhaust is impossible to match on two wheels anywhere.

But dreaming apart, even in these days when four-cylinder sports bikes are commonplace, the MV has plenty to offer, despite a price tag that can approach £4,000 when all the standard extras are optioned for.

With these, which include a fairing, rear disc brake and magnesium-alloy cast wheels, and the 812 cc engine conversion that boosts power to around 100 bhp for a top speed of 140 mph, the price goes well over £4,000!

Designed originally for the United States

market – as the name suggests – the 750S America is also the biggest MV ever sold. Standard capacity is 790 cc enabling MV to provide extra flexibility over the previous 750 cc models.

As it was aimed strictly at the USA market, the America offers a degree of civility and manners unseen on an MV before. Not only does the big four provide scintillating performance and handling but also it does so now with more comfort, less sound (although what is still there is just as spine chilling as ever), and without possibility of sucking dirt that the old seven-fifties were able to do. The 750S America has an air filter, one that would not look out of place on a mass-produced Japanese multi.

Tested by *Motor Cycle* at MIRA, the big MV recorded a top speed of 120 mph, an achievement that would have been bettered by some 10 mph had the 1,500-yd confines of the timing strip not conspired against the machine's high gearing. As it was, the 750S was still accelerating in top gear as it passed through the timing lights.

In the 812 cc 850 Monza form, achieved by boring out the cylinders, fitting hairier camshafts and bigger pistons and dispensing with the air filter and restrictive silencers, the MV was much faster.

On the timing strip it clocked a mean 130 mph, but with a longer run in on the mile-long straights at MIRA achieved 144 mph in one direction with the rider flat on the tank for a

The MV Agusta 750S America can be obtained in standard trim (left), or with all the extras (far left), that include magnesium alloy wheels, a disc rear brake and a full fairing. Further options can boost engine power to over 100 bhp and top speed to 140 mph

Specification

Engine: 790 cc (67 × 56 mm) double-overhead camshaft, transverse, in-line four. Light-alloy cylinder head and barrels; cast-iron liners. Six roller main bearings; needle roller big ends. Wet sump lubrication; gear pump. Compression ratio, 9·5 to 1. Four 26-mm choke VHB Delorto carburettors with lever-operated cold-start jets; foam element air filter. Maximum claimed power, 75 bhp at 8,500 rpm. Maximum torque, 48 lb-ft at 7,500 rpm.

Transmission: Primary helical gears. Wet, multiplate clutch and five-speed gearbox. Overall ratios: 11·84, 8·4, 6·37, 5·52 and 4·97 to 1. Final drive by bevel gears and shaft. Mph at 1,000 rpm in top gear, 15·2.

Electrical Equipment: Coil and distributor ignition. 12-volt, 32-amp-hour battery and belt-driven 135-watt dc dynamo-starter. 7-in diameter headlamp with 60/55-watt halogen main bulb. Four fuses; direction indicators.

Brakes: Scarab 11-in diameter double disc front, 10-in diameter rear.

Tyres: Metzeler, 3·50 × 18-in ribbed front, 4·00 × 18-in C7 block rear. Cast magnesium-alloy wheels.

Suspension: Ceriani telescopic front fork. Pivoted rear fork with manual five-position spring preload adjustment.

Frame: Duplex tube cradle frame.

Dimensions: Wheelbase, 55 in; seat height, 30 in; ground clearance, 7 in; handlebar width, 28 in; castor angle, 63°; trail, 3·2 in; turning circle, 17 ft 9 in; all unladen.

Weight: 510 lb including one gallon of fuel.

Fuel Capacity: 4·2 UK gal (5 US gal) including 7 pt reserve.

Sump Oil Capacity: 6·6 pt.

Manufacturer: Meccanica Verghera SpA, viale Adriatico 50, 21010 Verghera (Varese).

Performance

Maximum Speeds (Mean): 120·2 mph; 115·7 mph with rider sitting normally.
Best One-way Speed: 122·1 mph – dry track, slight tail wind.
Braking Distance – from 30 mph: 28 ft 9 in.
Fuel Consumption: 46·1 miles/UK gal (38·3 miles/US gal).
Oil Consumption: 750 mpp.
Minimum Non-snatch Speed: 23 mph in top gear.
Speedo Accuracy:

Indicated mph	30	40	50	60	70	80	90
Actual mph	29·6	38·6	47·7	57·4	67·2	77·7	88·6

mean two-way figure of 140 mph.

On the road there is no denying the MV's heritage. Crouched down behind the fairing the sensations are just the same as being on a racer.

The screen is wrapped tightly around the nose of the bike without a millimetre to spare and the engine below you produces all the busy racket of a unit built with dozens of ball and roller bearings to run with minimum friction.

Snap the throttles in neutral and the motor reacts with an immediate, momentous whoop. Do it with 6,000 already showing on the rev counter in top gear and it thrusts you forward with contemptuous ease.

The four slides on the 26-mm choke VHB Delorto carbs are controlled by a single cable and, like all the controls, operate with maximum co-operation for the rider.

The MV is a machine that makes no excuses for itself. And finished in bright red with a black suede seat that can accommodate two by moving the rear section back 3 inches, it lacks nothing but subtlety.

Based on the 500 cc four-cylinder racing design of the 1950s and 1960s, the double-overhead camshaft engine could never be mass produced. Beautifully cast in satin finished alloy, the crankcases are a one-piece casting into which the crankshaft assembly, separate cylinder barrels and one-piece head are bolted. Every shaft is supported in either roller or ball bearings and the cams are driven by a train of gears between the centre cylinders.

One of the pleasures of running the MV is starting it up in the morning and identifying all the variety of sounds coming from it.

The starting and generating system is unique. To keep the engine slim (it is as narrow as most twins) the combined starter-generator is driven by a pair of belts beneath the gearbox. With a massive 32-amp-hour battery to power the starter, it never baulked even in frosty weather. But the engine is naturally cold blooded and took several miles to warm up.

Only real concession to road use in the transmission is the shaft final drive. Otherwise the five-speed gearbox is pure competition style, the gearchange losing nothing in being switched to the left-hand side and snicking through the ratios with the precision of a camera shutter.

The only dubious aspect of the drive train is the clutch. For although it was impressivly light in action and smooth in taking up the drive, it swelled badly after being slipped when getting off the mark in acceleration tests. Nevertheless, with a bottom gear giving 58 mph at 9,000 rpm, there was sufficient power to lift the front wheel and push the bike to 60 mph in under 5 sec!

Over 30 mph the MV handles very well. At low speeds the weight and riding position give a slight unwieldy feeling, but the opposite is true once the machine is given its head. The steering tautens, improving with speed and the bike becomes utterly secure. Between 80 mph and 100 mph the MV is rock steady and the combination of a very responsive engine, minimal vibration, a

The MV Agusta four-cylinder engine is very slim from the use of a dynamo beneath the gearbox and an ignition distributor behind the cylinders

superb high speed riding position and one of the greatest sounds in motor cycling is an experience difficult to beat.

It is not the sort of bike you could recommend for long distance riding though. The Ceriani suspension is very hard and while offering good control for a bike of the MV's weight gives a rough ride over anything but the smoothest of surfaces. High speed cornering is secure but the ground clearance wanting, as the side and main stands touch down very easily. With two discs on the front wheel and one on the rear, the braking is a model of perfection. Made by either Scarab or Brembo, the discs are in cast iron with light-alloy double-acting calipers. At any speed, the slightest touch of the hand lever or foot pedal gives instant action without fear of locking the wheels. The brakes work very well in the wet too.

In its 790 cc form, the MV is fairly economical to run, giving an average 46 mpg which with the 4·2 gallon fuel tank gives a reasonable range of 190 miles, a distance greater than can be comfortably managed anyway because of the hard springing. However, with hard use, the consumption can drop to 35 mpg and in the 812 cc form this can go as low as 30 mpg. In either form, high octane fuel is imperative.

The MV Agusta 750S America and the 850 Monza are bikes for the committed and wealthy connoisseur. Many Japanese machines can provide similar specifications and even have better performance, but none can compare to the MV's quality of sight and sound. The MV is to be ridden *and* experienced. And with the America having thrown off its previous reputation for having poor detailing and finish, it has risen to being one of the true classic motor cycles.

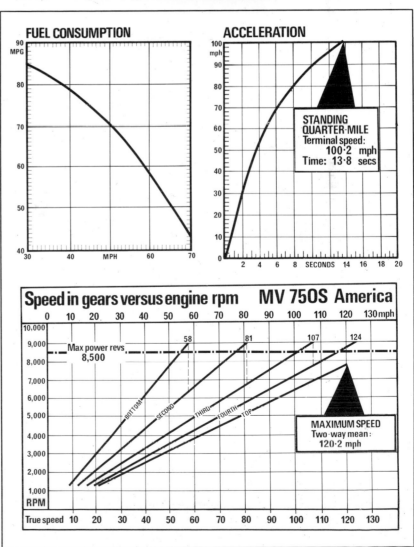

FUEL CONSUMPTION

ACCELERATION

STANDING
QUARTER-MILE
Terminal speed:
100·2 mph
Time: 13·8 secs

Speed in gears versus engine rpm **MV 750S America**

Max power revs 8,500

58   81   107   124

BOTTOM SECOND THIRD FOURTH TOP

MAXIMUM SPEED
Two-way mean:
120·2 mph

Norton Commando 850 Mk 3

Irony always accompanied the Norton Commando. Introduced in the late 1960s as a smooth and refined version of the traditional big British twin, its essential character was one dear to the heart of the enthusiast fond of the basic values in motor cycles. It was fast, lusty, lithe and light and virtues such as easy starting and quietness didn't fit into the conception.

The early 750 cc models were quick, with top speeds close to 120 mph and a combination of blinding acceleration and flexibility that has rarely been matched. Then the 828 cc models which were introduced in 1973 in an effort to improve reliability proved even better. They were tough, handled well and using Norton's patented rubber mountings for the engine and transmission were very smooth at high speed.

But the tough American noise regulations and a desire to appeal to a wider market spelled the end for the performance image. Three years later, the final form of the Commando, the Mark 3, appeared with electric starting, better comfort, disc brakes on both wheels and barely a whisper from the exhaust.

The irony was that when the Commando finally competed successfully against the Japanese competition in refinement, financial problems at the manufacturers, Norton-Villiers-Triumph, led to the end of its production in favour of the Triumph Trident, which was regarded as a more modern machine. The last Commando Mark 3 eight-fifties were completed

in early 1977 while the Marston Road, Wolverhampton, factory was in the hands of the Official Receiver. The penalty that was paid for the civilized nature of those last Nortons was in acceleration. While the early Commandos weighed around 440 lb, the last Mark 3 versions tipped the scales at over 500 lb, enough to add a second to the standing quarter-mile times. With a time of 14·4 sec and a terminal speed of 90 mph it was little better than most 550 cc machines of the day.

The appeal of the Commando lay in its instant engine response. The layout of the engine and transmission with the 828 cc long-stroke parallel twin and separate four-speed gearbox was straight from the 1950s. Major differences were that the triplex chain primary drive had in the final form a tensioner and, as on the original Commandos, an all-metal diaphragm spring clutch.

The engine itself, with a bore and stroke of 77 mm by 89 mm, has a crankshaft with two roller main bearings and with a compression ratio of 8 to 1 was in a very soft state of tune. Developing 52 bhp at 6,000 rpm, it was as unobtrusive as an engine could be yet packed a punch from low revs that made the gearbox almost unnecessary.

The bike was still able to cruise comfortably and smoothly at 90 mph, but much of the old liveliness had been lost. Unlike the older eight-fifties, which would rev safely to over 7,000 rpm, the Mark 3 is at its best between 2,000 and 4,000 rpm. It pulls hard from 1,500 but beyond 6,000 the restrictive air intake and exhaust silencing cuts the power drastically. And there is no point at all in revving to 6,500 rpm.

Normally, such a lazy and relaxing type of power delivery makes a bike easy and undemanding to ride, and this is true up to a point on the Mark 3.

The four-speed gearbox complements the engine well and the drive is delightfully smooth, the rubber vane dampers in the rear wheel, added to ease the load on the gearbox, giving a snatch-free ride at no more than a walking pace in bottom gear. But the overall gearing is very high with a top gear ratio of 4·18 to 1. This, the optimum gearing for the engine, giving 6,000 rpm when the rider is flat on the tank at the top speed of 115 mph. At 70 mph, the unit is ticking over at a modest 3,800 rpm. The motor never feels that it is working hard, and there is never anything that could be called vibration at motorway cruising speeds.

However, the characteristics of the rubber engine mounting system made slow riding a chore. While the rubber units absorb the vibration at normal engine revs, an inescapable feature of the system is that it resonates at certain rev bands. On the Commando this is at 2,000 rpm. With the high gearing this occurs at 40 mph in top gear (a perfectly feasible speed for the torquey engine). The rider has to keep changing gear just to avoid the resonant vibrations. Fortunately the gear change is very good. None could be more creamy or positive in action, even though the lever has been transferred to the left-hand side of the bike.

In their day Norton Commandos were unbeatable in production machine racing and even in its final form the Mark III 850 cc twin exhibited the same legendary handling

Another poor aspect of town riding was a result of weak carburation, most obvious in throttle response where it showed as an occasional spit back through the two 30-mm choke Amal Concentric carburettors. The idling mixture control was near perfect, giving an excellent 500 rpm idling speed even after a brisk run; a period of slow running in town heated up the carbs enough to cause stalling. This was not the

headache in traffic that it used to be – just a touch of the green twistgrip-mouthed button and the electric starter spins the engine back into life.

It is not always like that – from cold, the Amal carbs still need messy flooding and the starter motor occasionally baulks at turning the engine over against compression without momentum from the crank's massive flywheel. And although we are assured of its normality, the crunching of the backfire-overload device when the engine stops sounds horrible. Such things are easily forgotten once you take the Commando for a cross-country spin. For like the Triumph Trident, the Norton Commando's handling is just great. The steering is neutral throughout the speed range and flicking into a bend needs no more than a nudge. Moreover, the bike feels absolutely secure when cranked over with the footrests lightly skimming the tarmac.

The other side of the coin is the poor ride quality of the stiff suspension. Small ripples are transmitted undiminished to the rider's hands and once caused the front wheel to step out in a bend. Only the bigger bumps are absorbed.

In this the Commando is no better and no worse than most contemporary bikes, although the deeper seat Norton use to absorb the bumps in fact spoils the comfort of the machine.

Without moving back the footrests to suit the long tank of the Interstate version (the test model), too much weight is placed on the rider's behind at speed and he wallows around on the padding. The seat cover is too thin, too, and under full acceleration the seat pan slipped and ripped through the material at the front.

Commando braking can be very good, especially now with the disc rear brake. The front brake lever is neatly curved to fit the hand and the power is immense. The rear unit was spoilt by an out-of-true disc and a leaking master cylinder.

Likewise the electrics of the bike are good with an exceptionally powerful 60-watt H4 quartz-

Specification

Engine: 828 cc (77 × 89 mm) overhead valve, parallel twin. Light-alloy head. Two caged-roller main bearings; plain big ends. Dry sump lubrication. Compression ratio, 8·5 to 1. Two 32-mm Amal carburettors with handlebar lever operated cold-start slides; washable oil-soaked air filter. Claimed maximum power, 58 bhp at 5,900 rpm.

Transmission: Triplex primary chain. Wet, multiplate clutch with diaphragm spring and four-speed gearbox. Overall ratios: 10·71, 6·84, 5·1 and 4·18 to 1. Final drive by 0·625 × 0·375-in chain. Mph at 1,000 rpm in top gear, 20.

Electrical Equipment: Twin coil ignition with ballast resistor. 12-volt, 13-amp-hour battery and 120-watt alternator with twin Zener diode charge control. 7-in diameter headlamp with 60/55-watt halogen main bulb. Starter motor, direction indicators, headlamp flasher, accessory terminal.

Brakes: Hydraulically-operated 10·7-in diameter disc front and rear.

Tyres: Dunlop K81, 4·10 × 19 in front and rear.

Suspension: Telescopic front fork. Pivoted rear fork with three-position spring preload adjustment. Girling dampers.

Frame: Duplex tube frame with 2-in spine and rubber suspension for engine-transmission unit.

Dimensions: Wheelbase, 57 in; seat height, 32 in; ground clearance, 6 in; overall length, 88 in; turning circle, 18 ft 6 in; all unladen.

Weight: 486 lb with one gallon of fuel.

Fuel Capacity: 5·2 UK gal (6·2 US gal) including about 6 pt reserve.

Oil Tank Capacity: 5·25 pt.

Manufacturer: Norton Villiers Ltd, Marston Road, Wolverhampton.

Performance

Maximum Speeds (Mean): 114·9 mph; 96·9 mph with rider in two-piece outfit sitting normally.

Best One-way Speed: 115·4 mph – dry track, slight cross wind.

Braking Distance – from 30 mph: 28 ft.

Fuel Consumption: 43·2 miles/UK gal (35·9 miles/US gal) overall.

Oil Consumption: 700 mpp overall.

Minimum Non-snatch Speed: 16 mph in top gear.

Speedo Accuracy:

Indicated mph	30	40	50	60	70	80	90	100
Actual mph	30·3	40·6	50·9	61·2	71·5	82·5	93·4	104·3

Besides being dated with its long-stroke pushrod engine and separate gearbox, the performance of the Commando was spoilt by restrictive silencing and the extra weight of equipment like electric starting to satisfy the American market

halogen headlamp offering a sharp pencil main beam and a well cut-off dip. The switchgear and controls are equal to anything on a Japanese machine. The clutch lever pull is light and smooth while all the necessary switches are in easy reach.

Maintenance has been eased on the latest 850, too, the most significant modification being the use of easily adjustable rubber engine/transmission mountings. Since the rear-wheel fork was mounted to the rear of the gearbox plates, excessive side play affected the handling adversely. This used to be adjusted for side clearance with steel shims – a very time-consuming job that brought criticism for the amount of attention it needed to keep the handling in trim. The final models used a much more sensible screw adjustment that requires the use of a small tool in the kit. It takes barely half an hour to set it up to taste, balancing vibrations from the transmission against handling quality.

The primary chain is adjusted automatically instead of moving the gearbox to tension the chain, and the rear wheel really is quickly detachable.

Overall fuel consumption averaged 44 mpg, but a tune-up and tappet adjustment (just like the old days) before the MIRA test session improved this to 51 mpg for the final tankful. Oil used improved to 700 mpp at 1,800 miles from new.

In its Manx Norton-type finish of silver with red and black lining, the Commando is as handsome as ever with plenty of polished alloy and chrome.

It is sad that production of the Commando was stopped so soon with such a loyal following of riders.

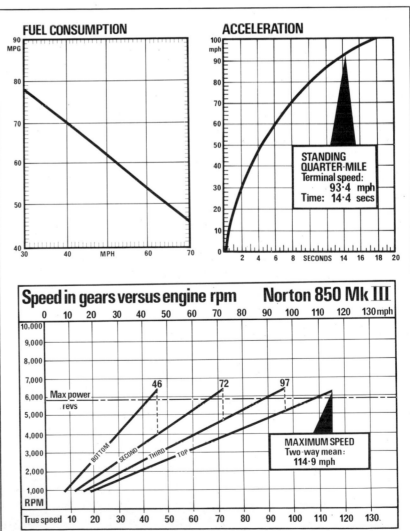

FUEL CONSUMPTION

ACCELERATION

STANDING QUARTER-MILE
Terminal speed: 93·4 mph
Time: 14·4 secs

Speed in gears versus engine rpm   **Norton 850 Mk III**

Max power revs

46   72   97

BOTTOM   SECOND   THIRD   TOP

MAXIMUM SPEED
Two-way mean:
114·9 mph

Suzuki GT750M

Suzuki, like Kawasaki, were slow to produce a large capacity roadster in answer to Honda's CB750 four. But when they did, early in 1972, it was a stunner. As expected of a factory with an already strong line of two-strokes and a reputation for thorough design and conservative styling, the Suzuki GT750 was an extension of the theme but with new twists that gave the bike a definite edge.

It was a three-cylinder machine, like the Kawasaki 750 that appeared the same year, but from there on the two machines diverged in completely opposite directions. Where the Kawasaki was a harsh, untamed and indecently fast, the Suzuki sniffed back with the grand touring image that its model number suggested. It was big, bulky, luxurious and gentlemanly; a machine for quiet and unobtrusively fast travel.

It was also uniquely Suzuki. Today we accept that the big four Japanese manufacturers produce very similar machines in a variety of classes. But in 1972 each factory was able to follow its own style; Suzuki's was the development of the sophisticated two-stroke engine, and in the GT750 they took it to the limit.

With all three cylinders housed in a jacket, the GT750 engine was liquid cooled with a massive radiator spanning the front of the engine, the liquid being circulated by a mechanical pump in the bottom of the broad crankcases. To make the engine narrower, the porting was canted to one side, giving an asymmetric appearance to the three exhaust pipes.

To give the engine and cycle parts a slim

Below: the Suzuki GT750M was much faster than the earlier water-cooled threes but still needed respect on twisty roads
Far right: the GT750A had slightly restyled tank graphics

waistline, the gearbox was narrowed by taking the drive from the built-up crankshaft by gears on the inner side of the right-hand side cylinder. Lubrication was Suzuki's patented system with a gearbox-driven pump supplying the cylinder walls and main bearings with oil from a tank under the seat. To allow for variations in load, the oil input was varied according to the throttle opening, a cable from the twistgrip altering the throw of the pump.

For the ruggedness of its engineering, the big Suzuki was modestly tuned. Three 32-mm choke carburettors fed the simple porting and on a corrected compression ratio of 6·7 to 1 the 738 cc engine developed a claimed 67 bhp at 6,500 rpm. How accurate that figure was is neither here nor there, for the great virtue of the GT750 was its flexibility. With a muted drone from the four exhaust pipes (the middle cylinder fed a bifurcated pair of silencers underneath the two outer pipes), the big Suzy would pull like a train from low revs and this made the five-speed gearbox rather superfluous. But it was all in character. The suspension was soft and mushy and the limited ground clearance afforded by the bulky exhaust system further discouraged spirited cornering.

It was slow too, an aspect of the bike that was to stand out for some time despite the successful racing efforts of the factory using tuned versions of the engine developing over 100 bhp and capable of over 170 mph.

In a period when most seven fifties were capable of reaching nearly 120 mph, the GT750 was unable to top 110 mph and its weight (nearly 550 lb) prevented startling acceleration. Neither was its fuel consumption impressive.

Run the bike at anything like its maximum cruising speed of 90 mph, which it would be able to do smoothly and reliably for as long as the rider could manage the rather ungainly riding position, and the three big 32-mm choke Mikuni carburettors would guzzle fuel at an alarming rate; 30 mpg would not be unusual and this drawback was only partially overcome by the size of the fuel tank. In these days when disc brakes are becoming increasingly criticised for their poor wet performance, the stopping equipment on the early GT750s would please many a long-distance tourer; a double-leading shoe, double-sided drum unit no less! But it failed to meet the promise of its appearance and repeated stops from speed would provoke fade easily.

Apart from boosting the braking power with a pair of massive discs on the front wheel (albeit with a disclaimer stuck to the front fork warning of the delay in their wet weather potency), Suzuki appeared rather happy for the GT750 to retain its podgy character for three years.

With the introduction of the GT750M in 1975 that all changed. Suddenly here was a Suzuki that could take on the best superbikes and come out on top. Compared to the old model it looked crisp, lean and hungry, although it was still a formidable machine for fast riding. Porting changes, which were the most significant modifi-

cations to the bike, boosted the power to 70 bhp at 6,500 rpm. Gone was the electric fan behind the radiator (meant for tropical climates only) and the exhaust system was cleaned up and more tidily tucked into the running gear. Three massive 40-mm choke constant-velocity carburettors with a single control cable allowed deeper breathing for the chunky motor.

The alterations had had the desired effect, transforming the podgy tourer into a drag strip flyer. In its new guise, the GT750 wound up to 120 mph mean top speed on test and sprinted through the standing quarter-mile in 13·5 sec, terminating at 100 mph.

This increase in performance was achieved with little sacrifice of the bike's high-speed touring character. The GT750 is as tireless, smooth and comfortable as ever. Better still, the fuel consumption was improved. Although one of the better two-strokes in this respect, and even though most of the test mileage was clocked on motorways, overall consumption during our test was 45 mpg, while the lowest figure recorded – during the flat out MIRA test session – was a remarkable 40 mpg. And all on low-grade fuel too.

But while the engine has been improved with lengthened port timing, bigger constant-velocity Mikuni carburettors, higher compression ratio and the overall gearing raised, the chassis has remained little changed. The handling has not kept pace with the increased performance; this is not too great a problem as the cornering clearance, although vastly improved since the earlier models, still puts the dampers on any

spirited riding. The GT750 now has an identity crisis too. The bike still looks a podgy tourer with its massive silencers, four in all, and this could have discouraged potential customers although the bike represented the best value for money in th 750 cc class, considering its all-round performance.

It could also put them off experiencing one of the more thrilling seven fifties. Blip the lightweight throttle and the crank spins instantaneously in response. The flywheels are so light and the engine so free moving that it sounds and feels more like a small two-stroke twin.

Suzy will hold it for you as long as you want. Even at high speeds the 750 has a range of 155 miles before reserve, and more with the bigger tank of the later GT750A. And at these sort of speeds there is plenty in hand. Just a shade off the stop is needed to maintain 70 mph and at 5,000 rpm (90 mph) in top tweaking the grip produces a healthy kick for overtaking.

Except for a pronounced chain noise at speed, engine noise levels are remarkably low too, but engine vibration intrudes into the picture above 70 mph sufficiently to buzz the footrests and send the rider's feet to sleep. This is in spite of the three-cylinder engine, which by nature produces a side to side rocking vibration, being mounted in rubber bushes. In general use this vibration goes unnoticed apart from around the marked resonance period at 7,000 rpm, when the shaking is clearly visible.

Starting and idling belie the Suzuki's high power capabilities. Without a sound it responds instantly to the starter button and relaxes into a reliable, if slightly irregular sounding tickover (difficult to persuade down to 1,000 rpm without putting up with the occasional stalling).

The clutch is as smooth and light as ever but the gearbox has the same annoying Suzuki characteristics. Bottom gear was rarely engaged noiselessly, particularly if the rear chain needed adjustment, and selection of the lower ratios nearly always felt clonky. Otherwise the gearbox, which has had the top two ratios closed up so that there is now only a 1,200 rpm drop between the two, felt perfectly crisp. Particularly useful for telling a rider he has reached top gear is the digital gear indicator in the instrument console. As each ratio is selected then the relative number is shown. If this not necessarily a must for a modern bike it does indicate the level to which Suzuki has refined its instrumentation.

Both the 160 mph speedo and rev counter are lit at night by a cosy green glow; between them are the warning lights and water temperature gauge, which never wavered over 'cool'.

Controls have never been bettered on a Suzuki. As for the overall comfort of the bike, the hand controls have been refined to the point where they are no longer noticed. What is needed is there, instantly, but I would prefer control levers that were thicker, particularly for the brake lever as this requires heavy pressure, although it was good to see the rubber cover over the cable end.

In spite of the very wide engine (28 in) the riding comfort is good. The seat is long and wide and the flat handlebar gives the rider a good stance at high speed while remaining relaxed at low speed.

The suspension could be improved however. While the front fork has a pleasantly soft but slightly underdamped action, the rear suspension units transmitted too much of the small road ripples and were overdamped. The effect was very annoying over badly surfaced roads as practically everything was transmitted to the rider while the bigger bumps only were absorbed.

Specification

Engine: 738 cc (70 × 64 mm) water-cooled, two-stroke, in-line three. Linered light-alloy cylinder block and head. Four ball main bearings; needle-roller big ends. Lubrication by throttle-controlled pump to main bearings and cylinder bores. Compression ratio, 6·9 to 1 (from exhaust port closure). Three 40 mm Mikuni CV carburettors with lever-operated cold-start jets; paper element air filter. Claimed maximum power 70 bhp at 6,500 rpm.
Transmission: Primary helical gears. Wet, multiplate clutch and five-speed gearbox. Overall ratios: 12·8, 7·81, 6·13, 5·06 and 4·33 to 1. Final chain, 0·625 × 0·375 in. Mph at 1,000 rpm in top gear, 17.
Electrical Equipment: Coil ignition. 12-volt, 14-amp-hour battery and 280-watt excited field alternator and voltage regulator. 6·5-in headlamp with 50/40-watt main bulb. Starter motor; direction indicators; headlamp flasher; gear position indicator.
Brakes: Hydraulically-operated twin 11·75 in diameter front discs; 7·5 in drum rear.
Tyres: Avon Roadrunner, 4·10 × 19 in front, 4·10 × 18 in rear.
Suspension: Telescopic front fork. Pivoted rear fork with three-position spring preload adjustment.
Frame: Welded duplex tube with pressed plate gusseting.
Dimensions: Wheelbase, 58·75 in; seat height, 31 in; ground clearance, 6 in; all unladen.
Weight: Approximately 550 lb.
Fuel Capacity: 3·75 UK gal (4·5 US gal) including reserve.
Oil Tank Capacity: 3·2 pt.
Manufacturer: Suzuki Motor Co., 300 Takatsuka, Hamamatsu, Japan.

Performance

Maximum Speeds (Mean): 119·8 mph; 110·2 mph with rider seated normally.
Best One-way Speed: 120·4 mph – dry track, hot with slight cross wind.
Braking Distance – from 30 mph: 30 ft 6 in.
Fuel Consumption: 45·3 miles/UK gal (37·6 miles/US gal).
Oil Consumption: 348 mpp overall.
Minimum Non-snatch Speed: 14 mph in top gear.
Speedo Accuracy:

Indicated mph	20	30	40	50	60	70	80	90	100
Actual mph	19	28·6	37·6	46·5	55·6	64·7	74·4	84	93·8

With the new porting the power characteristics have been completely transformed. What was formerly a tourquey engine is now a revver. Little power is developed below 4,000 rpm, although it will pull usefully for town work. Opening the throttles produces little more than a moan from the air filter, but as the revs build up and reach 4,000 rpm the bike shoots forward and the engine whirrs like a turbine as the maximum power revs at 6,500 rpm are reached.

With such a reduction in flexibility you might expect the touring ability of the Suzuki to be hampered. But the gearbox ratios – apart from the large gap from bottom to second where the revs drop from 7,000 to 4,200 – are adequately close when the gear pedal is used vigorously.

The high-speed cruising character of the GT750, one of its great strengths, has also not been lost in the change. Just attain the speed you want – anything up to 100 mph – and the big

Tough emission regulations in America have outlawed the smooth and silky Suzuki 750 three in favour of the cleaner running four-stroke GS750 four

Avon Roadrunner tyres were fitted front and rear instead of the standard Bridgestones. If anything, they improved the steering at low speeds due to the large rolling diameter of the tyre increasing the self-centring action. The steering lightens as you lean the bike over and move onto the more curved section of the tread on the side walls, a characteristic which was unnerving at first. In addition, the whole machine feels less than stable at anything over 90 mph.

There is also a ground clearance problem. The silencers have been lifted up but the wide main and prop stands still crunch down at only moderate lean angles.

In contrast the braking is superb. The twin power at the expense of heavy lever action . . . in the dry. What happens in the wet at slow speeds in unknown as it never rained during the test, but Suzuki are obviously aware of some shortcomings and they say so by warning owners with a sticker on the front fork leg. It is just as well there is a decent drum rear brake.

Lighting, which does not include a pilot bulb in the headlamp, is ample for the legal limit.

The tools are sufficient for the tasks most owners will use them for, the only attention our test bike needing being to lift the seat and refill the oil tank, the lubricant for which was used at 350 miles to the pint, giving a range of over 1,000 miles, and one adjustment of the rear chain in the same period.

The GT750, which was dropped from the Suzuki range at the end of 1977, was a healthy alternative to the faster four-stroke GS750 four, even if dated in its handling and comfort. Had it not been for exhaust emission control laws it might still be with us.

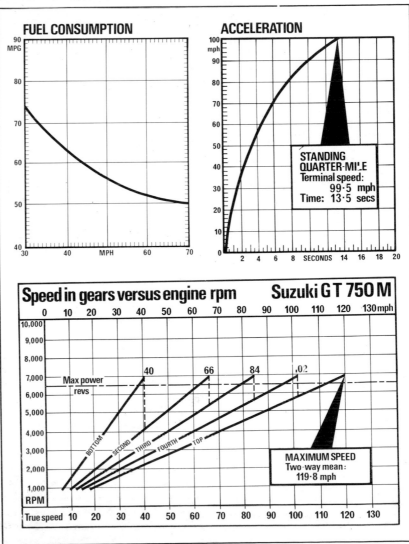

FUEL CONSUMPTION

ACCELERATION

STANDING QUARTER-MILE
Terminal speed:
99·5 mph
Time: 13·5 secs

Speed in gears versus engine rpm — Suzuki GT 750 M

Max power revs

BOTTOM SECOND THIRD FOURTH TOP

MAXIMUM SPEED
Two-way mean:
119·8 mph

Suzuki RE5

With the generally overwhelming success of the Japanese motor cycle industry it is all too easy to forget the disasters. For there were the lemons, and along with Yamaha's ill-fated and unreliable TX750 ohc twin, Suzuki's foray into the rotary-engine field with the RE5 was the most disastrous of the lot.

We write of the RE5 in the past tense because after its introduction in late 1974, production lasted only two years and with slight simplifications in the specification faultered toward its

demise in mid-summer 1977.

By all the criteria, the RE5 was a superbike, despite all its faults. It was big, smooth and if not actually capable of blinding acceleration through the quarter mile, offered the rider a flexible engine and short-burst super-smooth high speed cruising.

The main reasons for its failure were fundamental as well as obvious. Outlandish it certainly was, too outlandish in appearance and sound. But basically it could not deliver the goods. Its performance profile almost mirrored the cheaper GT550 two-stroke three while offering nothing more in excitement and image.

Four years of development went into Japan's first entry into the rotary-bike arena and Suzuki's first attack into the ultra-luxury bike field. Millions of miles in conditions that varied from arctic to desert were covered during the factory road testing period.

Suzuki obviously had considerable confidence in it, for they invested millions in the programme along with a new factory specially built for the sole purpose of rotary production.

Anything but a remarkable machine from such massive investment would have come as a surprise, and the RE5 was certainly that. A combination of Italian and Japanese styling set off the massive alloy rotary engine-transmission unit that was tightly packed into the frame.

In typical Japanese fashion, Suzuki built into the RE5 every conceivable design feature to remove any possibility of criticism. Unfortunately, it resulted in an extremely heavy machine. Fully tanked up, it weighed a fantastic 5 cwt – 560 lb. Even with only one gallon of fuel it tipped the scales at more than the previously heaviest Jap machine, the Kawasaki 900 four. This is certainly remarkable when you remember the claims made for the Wankel engine during its infancy, of its relative compactness for a given capacity, light weight and smoothness.

There is no doubt about the rotary's virtues and of the Suzuki RE5 engine, particularly. As a motor cycle power unit, it was the silkiest, mechanically quietest and one of the most flexible yet seen.

More in line with contemporary Wankel-powered cars, the RE5 had a water-cooled casing for the motor and a cooling radiator very similar to the Suzuki GT750 two-stroke three. This also incorporated an electric fan, a feature dropped on the later model.

The rotor itself was cooled by the rotor shaft lubricant supplied by an Eaton-type pump from the sump under the engine unit, coolant circulating to an additional radiator beneath the water radiator.

The rotor tips were lubricated, two-stroke fashion, by a throttle-controlled pump supplied from a tank under the seat. Both lubricating systems used the same oil but were entirely separate from each other.

Transmission was by a duplex chain to a multiple plate clutch and the GT750 gearbox.

For a motor cycle powered by a unit supposed to be less complicated and more compact than equivalent multi-cylinder engines, the RE5 was frighteningly complex. The carburettor, for example, had two pairs of push-pull cables plus a cable for the oil pump. The whole carburettor assembly required exceptionally careful setting up for the best results.

Where the RE5 was best, it was head-and-shoulders above the competition. It could cruise, smooth as glass and silent as a whisper, at speeds around 100 mph.

For a seasoned motor cyclist this can be a really strange experience. Like the Norton-Triumph rotary prototype, the Suzuki added a new dimension to autobahn travel and the reductions the smoothness can make to rider fatigue over long periods are much more than one would expect.

Suzuki have always been aware of the need for rider comfort, as has been ably demonstrated by all their smaller machines, and they went even farther with the RE5. Even though it is a massive machine overall, the seat was low and slim and most people had no problems in putting both feet flat on the ground when stationary. Flattish handlebars and nicely placed footpegs, mounted just aft of the seat nose, completed the picture.

In contrast, you need to be a champion weight lifter to pull the bike up on to its main stand, so poorly arranged is the foot lever on the stand.

Although top end performance was less than stunning, since Suzuki's 750 three can easily outpace the RE5 over the quarter-mile, the Rotary impressed mainly for its stump-pulling power at low revs and wide range of flexibility.

Throttle response was startling at the maximum torque revs of 3,500 rpm and twisting the grip really stretched a rider's arms before he realised that the bike was whistling toward the red line at 7,000 rpm.

Such a wide range of engine torque made the useful top gear range very broad and had it not been for the high tickover speed of 1,500 rpm, it might have been even better. The pulling ability of the RE5 was so hard that it could comfortably take a 1-in-3 test hill at 1,500 rpm in bottom gear and pull away at little more than this.

This, more than anything, accentuated the unusual exhaust note emitted by the RE5. At speed, the massive silencers with the 'Ram Air' cooling injectors at the front ends damped out the sharp exhaust notes into a hollow hum that hardly turned an ear. Below 4,000 rpm, used quite often, the notes from the single rotor sounded more like a cross between a Norton ES2 single and a Villiers two-stroke. And the 'pokity-pokity' racket was particularly resonant when one was pulled up beside cars at traffic lights.

One regrettable feature of the complex carburettor set-up meant that the model we tested was slightly below par – not enough to affect the maximum performance, but sufficient to spoil the light-throttle response of the two carburettor chokes, one of 18-mm and the other of 32-mm, the smaller of which have small ports with later timing ports for better filling at low revs.

Up to about 40 per cent of twistgrip movement, the smaller choke opens with no effect on the larger at all and response is quite sluggish. From there, the main choke takes over and the engine becomes much more lively. The vacuum-operated constant-velocity 32-mm choke could be beaten by a slick wrist and the engine would cough. Such a lag was also apparent in the vacuum sensing of the over-run ignition that fires the plug at half speed to prevent rough running on closed throttle.

Far left: *the Suzuki Rotary RE5A was sold in limited numbers with many components similar to the two-stroke GT750 three. In its original form* (below) *it had futuristic styling*

Until the ignition cut in a fraction of a second after shutting the throttle, quite considerable engine braking effect showed, sometimes with a discernible squeal from the rear tyre in low gears.

But then there came a deathly silence when the engine ran on without any braking effect at all, a characteristic that needed getting used to.

For all its refinement, the Suzuki demonstrated appalling fuel consumption figures.

Specification

Engine: Single-rotor, transversely-mounted, Wankel type; water-cooled casing and oil-cooled rotor; 497 cc chamber volume. Rotorshaft lubricated by Eaton-type pump; sump capacity, 3·8 pt. Rotor tips lubricated by throttle-controlled pump; tank capacity, 3 pt. Compression ratio, 9·4 to 1. Mikuni HHD carburettor with 18 mm primary and 32 mm secondary ports; lever-operated choke; oil-soaked polyurethane air filter. Claimed maximum power, 62 bhp at 6,500 rpm.

Transmission: Primary drive by 0·375 in pitch double-row chain with automatic tensioner. Wet, multiplate clutch and five-speed gearbox. Overall ratios: 14·44, 8·81, 6·91, 5·71 and 4·68 to 1. Final drive by 0·75 × 0·375-in 630 chain with throttle-controlled pump lubrication. Mph at 1,000 rpm in top gear, 16·7.

Electrical Equipment: Capacitor-discharge assisted coil ignition. 12-volt, 24-amp-hour battery and 280-watt alternator. 7-in diameter headlamp with 50/40-watt main bulb. Direction indicators; starter motor; headlamp flasher; coolant temperature gauge.

Brakes: Hydraulically-operated 11·75-in diameter double-disc front; 7-in SLS drum rear.

Tyres: Inoue Grand High Speed, 3·25 × 19-in ribbed front, 4·00 × 18-in patterned rear; light-alloy rims.

Suspension: Telescopic front fork with two-way damping. Pivoted rear fork with five-position spring preload adjustment.

Frame: Duplex loop cradle.

Dimensions: Wheelbase, 59 in; seat height, 32 in; ground clearance, 7·5 in; overall length, 81 in; turning circle, 17 ft; all unladen.

Weight: 560 lb with one gallon of fuel.

Fuel Capacity: 3·6 UK gal (4·3 US gal) including reserve.

Manufacturer: Suzuki Motor Company, 300 Takatsuka, Hamamatsu.

Performance

Maximum Speed (Mean): 110 mph.
Best One-way Speed: 116 mph – damp track, strong three-quarter tail wind.
Braking Distance: Not taken due to damp track.
Fuel Consumption: 40 miles/UK gal (33·2 miles/US gal) overall.
Minimum Non-snatch Speed: 25 mph in top gear.
Speedo Accuracy:

Indicated mph	20	30	40	50	60	70	80	90	100
Actual mph	18	27	37	48	59	69	79	89	99

Overall, but including a large proportion of motorway running, the RE5 recorded 30 mpg, and even with careful throttle use it showed only 40 mpg.

That sort of figure might have been acceptable to a rich buyer but for the fact that capacity of the RE5 tank was only 3½ gallons. As a long distance tourer, the RE5 was sorely handicapped with a range of less than 110 miles. Moreover, the capacity before the reserve tap was needed was only 2½ gallons and we rarely went 90 miles before opening up again. This was necessary because the low fuel warning lamp came on while on reserve.

As well as refuelling, the bike needed filling up with oil in the two locations, the sump using oil at 400 mpp, and the tank at 530 mpp.

The transmission was not quite up to the same impressive standard as the engine. The gearbox and clutch were typically Suzuki, being nigh on perfect for lightness of action except for a clonkiness in the action in the lower gears.

But Suzuki opted for the same heavy ¾-in pitch chain as used on the Kawasaki 900. The main trouble was in the need to use a 14-tooth engine sprocket and this led to annoying vibrations in the 4,000 to 4,500 rpm range.

On smooth dry roads the RE5 steered as well as any machine out of Japan. Slow turns in side streets and feet-up coasts to a stop can be just as well accomplished as high-speed bend swinging. But the bike never gave the same degree of confidence in its handling qualities as equivalent machines and this must to some extent be blamed on its excessive weight and top heaviness.

The suspension had a short movement and gave a well-cushioned ride while at the same time transmitting small ripples, rather like an early Honda 750. But although well damped, the rear spring units found trouble in controlling the comparatively light rear end on bumpy corners.

The main criticism was of the weight distribution. Not only was the RE5 a heavy machine but the centre of gravity was high as well, and this was obvious to anyone who tried to manhandle the bike.

For no apparent reason, apart perhaps from cosmetics, the engine was placed very high up in the frame, and this coupled with a high and heavy cooling system provided plenty of top hamper to limit spirited riding. It also made riding in the wet a nightmare as the tyres were only average on wet surfaces.

Wet weather also took the bite out of the front double disc brake – a characteristic which should have been sorted out by a company with Suzuki's resources.

For all Suzuki's efforts in producing sophisticated and reliable electrical systems, the headlight was poor too. There was plenty of power from the plastic casing mounted unit but, like all the smaller models, the dip beam dazzled too much due to the lack of adequate cut-off.

The instrumentation and detail work were fantastic. The cylindrical casing housing the 160 mph speedo and 9,000 rpm rev counter had a

Far left: *the RE5's instrument console had a flip-up lid released when the ignition was switched on. In addition to the coolant temperature gauge and digital gear indicator there was a row of warning lamps for fuel level, oil level, neutral and main beam, which could be checked before firing up*
Left: *the unorthodox engine with its dual choke carburettor forward of the rotor casing*

transparent green cover released when the ignition key next to it was switched on the checkout position. When this was used, the circuits operating the various warning lamps were checked. The low fuel lamp, the low oil and oil pressure all came on alongside the turn-signal repeater, main beam and neutral bulbs.

Between the instruments are the gear-position indicator and the coolant temperature gauge, which only went above the mid position when running at speed in dense motorway traffic.

Starting was absolutely simple. There was no messing with the vacuum-operated fuel tap, the ignition switch was turned to the main position, the choke lever on the carburettor pressed down (it is overridden at operating temperature) and a dab on the starter button did the trick.

The basic styling was very pleasing but spoiled by the unnecessary harping on the rotary idea with round casings for the rear lamp, instruments and the side covers. But the detail work was good, and typified by the extensive use of cap screws, and neat light-alloy wheel rims.

As a serious motorcycle it is difficult to imagine where the Suzuki RE5 fitted into the picture. It was too heavy and not powerful enough to be a sports machine, yet at the same time its long distance touring potential was marred by the heavy fuel consumption and limited range. It was no doubt aimed at the American long distance tourer who would find the utter smoothness and comfort a boon, if he did not mind stopping for fuel every 100 miles.

Looked at in cold hard terms, the RE5 offered little more than the GT550 Suzuki three at the expense of greater weight and fuel consumption, so where was the progress in that?

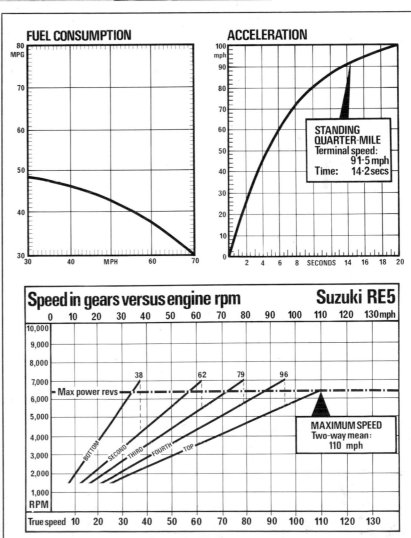

FUEL CONSUMPTION

ACCELERATION

STANDING QUARTER-MILE
Terminal speed: 91·5 mph
Time: 14·2 secs

Speed in gears versus engine rpm   **Suzuki RE5**

Max power revs

38   62   79   96

BOTTOM   SECOND   THIRD   FOURTH   TOP

MAXIMUM SPEED
Two-way mean: 110 mph

Suzuki GS750

With tough emmision controls in America pushing out Suzuki's top of the range water-cooled three-cylinder two-stroke GT750 at the end of 1977, the factory was bound to pull something exceptional out of the bag when they introduced their first large four-stroke machine. And when the four-cylinder GS750 appeared at the end of 1976, it proved to be not only the fastest seven-fifty on the market but the most compact and best mannered big bike to appear from Japan to that date. Most heavyweights are hard to handle when stationary and the Suzuki GS750 is no exception, but the factory engineers were bright enough to realise that what was needed in the 750 cc class was a machine with superior roadholding and manageability as well as more power.

What they came up with was a large motor cycle (60-in wheelbase) with uncanny stability for a Japanese bike at speed and with a remarkably low all-up weight of 510 lb when most 750 cc machines weighed around 540 lb. They mini-mised the effects of bulk by clever frame design that allowed a low seat height. The high power output of the engine developed a claimed 68 bhp at 8,500 rpm.

By the standards of the day – Honda later replied with their equally fast CB750F2 – the top speed of the GS750 was a revelation. Clocked at a mean two-way top speed of 124·3 mph it was

the fastest 750 cc machine ever tested by *Motor Cycle*.

Acceleration was no less stunning. Despite a poor rear tyre that limited traction in full-blooded drag style starts, the Suzuki catapulted to 60 mph from rest in under 4 sec – and can top 100 mph in under 13 sec.

For such performance the low overall fuel consumption is impressive too. Average for the test was just under 50 mpg while the bike was able to return 47 mpg when cruising at 70 mph on motorways.

Yet mechanically, the Suzuki is very conventional by contemporary standards. The four-cylinder 748 cc short stroke (65 by 56·4 mm) has double-overhead camshafts with chain drive and a built-up all-roller bearing crankshaft and gear primary drive that is a virtual copy of the Kawasaki 900 four, right down to valve sizes and the way inverted bucket followers with adjusting shims transmit camshaft thrust to the valves.

The frame is a well-braced duplex tube cradle and there is nothing radical or different about the suspension. Even the brakes follow fashion with a stainless-steel disc front and rear. But Suzuki have scored with the GS750 by absorbing every state-of-the-art idea on handling and rider comfort into the context of the classic Japanese multi. This shows immediately you slide into the seat. The machine is very low (31½ in unladen) and just as important, the seat is slim, along with the side panels, and is padded enough to prevent it knifing through you on long rides. Above all, the GS750 has a moulded-to-you feel that gives the rider confidence in the machine as soon as he is under way. And he will need it, for the Suzuki will out-accelerate just about anything on the road up to the legal limit.

Yet at low speeds, trundling around town, the way the bike can be weaved through the traffic belies none of the screaming performance and race-bred roadholding that befits a machine barely a few steps removed from Suzuki's world championship winning RG500 two-stroke road racer.

The steering and balance are as carefree as the controls are smooth and light, and the machine feels no heavier than the smaller Suzuki GT380 two-stroke. It makes the GS750 a joy to ride – unlike many Japanese heavyweights.

That is nothing compared to the thrill of cranking the big Suzy through fast bends. You feel as if you are piloting a responsive fighter aircraft. Squirt it, and the Suzy goes like a jet. Aim it and you have suddenly got an accurate missile in your hands.

The Suzuki engineers have tuned the steering so finely that it becomes taut at speed yet retains a useful amount of neutrality for flicking through corners with a minimal amount of effort from the rider.

While the steering geometry is certainly spot on, the frame itself contributes no less to the overall picture. Although very similar to the Kawasaki duplex frame, the Suzuki version is liberally gusseted around the steering head and

between the three top tubes for extra stiffness, while the swinging arm bearings are needle rollers to minimise wear and flexure.

It makes the Suzuki the scratcher's dream. The four exhaust pipes are routed into a single silencer on each side, and this offers cornering clearance which means that the Suzuki invites taste on normal roads.

Unfortunately the tyres and the rear suspension are not up to the standard of the rest of the running gear. The stock-issue Bridgestones are possibly long-lasting, but are the first to signal warnings on smooth surfaces, while the 120 lb/in rear springs are too hard for the dampers and start to bounce the rear end around on ripply tarmac. This is enough to provoke a slight side-to-side steering head motion above 90 mph.

The ride comfort suffers too, for even on apparently smooth roads the Suzuki bounces along perceptibly at the rear. Yet by comparison the front fork is superb. The soft 26/43 lb/in dual rate springs are just right and the fork gives a beautifully smooth ride; although the damping is apparently light, it works well in practice.

For long distance cruising the flat handlebar offers a neat riding posture that balances the wind pressure up to 80 mph. It would be even better with slightly more sweep on the handlebar and the footrests an inch or two further back.

Unless ridden hard with the engine revving to its 10,000 rpm limit, the Suzuki is commendably smooth too. Throughout the range, the engine

emits a high-frequency buzz which is at its worst when the motor is taken over 6,000.

It is much more comfortable than the two-stroke 750 cc Suzuki three and the other big four-stroke fours, although not quite up to the standard of a BMW or the Yamaha 750 cc three, except at 5,000 in top (around 70 mph) when it is mirror smooth.

Since the Suzuki's mirrors are rubber mounted they are never affected by vibration.

Average consumption was 46·7 mpg on the cheapest fuel with almost 55 mpg when ridden carefully, or a worst figure of 33 mpg at the test track.

Mechanical noise is low and flexibility is superb. At 30 mph in top it just hums along with no more than a slight hiss from the valve gear, but wind back the twistgrip and the bike will kick you straight up to a genuine 108 mph (115 mph indicated) without a single gearchange with the rider sitting bolt upright. With the rider flat on the tank, there is much more. Geared perfectly on its 5·6 to 1 top ratio the GS750 revved in top to 9,200 rpm, 300 rpm below the red line, for a two-way mean top speed of 124·3 mph.

Snap throttle is good provided there are more than 3,000 rpm on the tacho, below which the engine is perfectly tractable but unresponsive to full bore treatment.

The stunning road performance owes as much to the engine power as to the optium gearing used. The five-speed gearbox is as expected from Suzuki, slick, positive and noiseless, unless you try to perform quick changes at low engine revs, when it becomes a mite clunky. Overall gearing is comparatively low, and the buzzy feel of the engine often provoked the rider to feel for another gear ratio after top. The gear indicator in the instrument panel for once proved useful in this case. But the low gearing enhances the flexibility. In bottom gear, at 15·1 to 1 ratio, the bike will trickle along at little more than a casual walking pace, yet it tops out at 48 mph. The ratios are properly spaced, keeping the engine above peak torque revs (7,000 rpm) right through the range when revved to 9,500 rpm. But in everyday use the most useful gear is third which can leap the bike from 40 mph to 70 mph for instant overtaking.

The effect showed best at the test strip. Despite the lack of traction from the Bridgestone rear tyre, the Suzuki realed off a series of quarter-miles at 13·2 sec with a terminal speed of 103·5 mph.

Yet it came back with barely a ruffled feather. The clutch is light and smooth yet bites without a trace of slip, the exhaust pipes were as tarnish free as if they had just come off the spares shelf, and there was no trace of oil anywhere.

Braking during the tests at MIRA showed the Suzuki's 11¾-in discs to be very potent and fade-free from 30 mph in the dry with a stopping distance of under 26 ft. But in normal use they

Specification

Engine: 749 cc (65 × 56·4 mm) double-overhead camshaft, in-line, transverse four. Light-alloy cylinder head and block; cast-iron liners. Three roller and one ball main bearings; needle-roller big ends. Wet sump lubrication; trochoid pump. Compression ratio, 8·7 to 1. Four 26-mm choke Mikuni carburettors with lever-operated cold-start jets; oil-soaked foam air filter. Maximum claimed power, 68 bhp at 8,500 rpm. Maximum torque, 44 lb-ft at 7,000 rpm.
Transmission: Spur primary gears (ratio, 99/46). Wet, multiplate clutch and five-speed gearbox. Overall ratios: 15·1, 10·5, 8·12, 6·62 and 5·65 to 1. Final drive by 0·75 × 0·5-in roller chain (ratio 41/15). Mph at 1,000 rpm in top gear, 13·5.
Electrical Equipment: Twin coil ignition. 12-volt, 14-amp-hour battery and three-phase alternator with zener-diode voltage control. 7-in diameter headlamp with 50/40 watt main bulb. One fuse. Starter motor; direction indicators; gear position indicator.
Brakes: Hydraulically-operated 11·75-in diameter stainless-steel disc front and rear; single-piston caliper front, double rear.
Tyres: Bridgestone, 3·25H19 ribbed 21 F2 front, 4·00H18 patterned 21 R2 rear.
Suspension: Telescopic front fork; 6·3 in travel. Pivoted rear fork; spring damper units with 3·3 in travel, and five-position preload adjustment.
Frame: Welded duplex tube cradle.
Dimensions: Wheelbase, 59 in; seat height, 31·5 in; ground clearance, 7 in; handlebar width, 29 in; castor angle, 63°; trail, 4·2 in; turning circle, 15 ft 10 in; all unladen.
Weight: 510 lb including one gallon of fuel.
Fuel Capacity: 4 UK gal (4·8 US gal) including 4 pt reserve.
Sump Oil Capacity: 6·5 pt.
Manufacturer: Suzuki Motor Co. Ltd., 300 Takatsuka, Hamamatsu.

Performance

Maximum Speeds (Mean): 124·3 mph; 108·4 with normally-seated rider in two-piece over-suit.
Best One-way Speed: 125·3 mph – dry track, no wind.
Braking Distance – from 30 mph: 25 ft 6 in on dry tarmac.
Fuel Consumption: 46·7 miles/UK gal (38·8 miles/US gal).
Oil Consumption: 600 mpp.
Minimum Non-snatch Speed: 15 mph in top gear.
Speedo Accuracy:

Indicated mph	30	40	50	60	70	80	90
Actual mph	26·6	35·3	44·1	52·3	60·5	72·0	83·7

Like the Kawasaki Z1000, the Suzuki GS750 has double overhead cams and a roller and ball bearing crankshaft with gear drive to the clutch and five-speed gearbox. The 1,000 cc version recently introduced is no wider and in fact shorter and lighter than the seven fifty

were generally poor. The rear disc was far too insensitive from higher speeds and tended to overheat causing hopping of the rear wheel. Both brakes exhibited lag when used in heavy rain, the usual fault of stainless-steel discs.

Instrumentation and lighting were only average on the GS750. Speedometer and rev counter are in a new-style package that cants each instrument towards the rider's view. Unusually, they had red illumination which became distracting after a while. A higher standard of accuracy from the needles would have been preferable. The headlamp sends out a strong beam and the dip cut off is much better than Suzukis in the past. The left switch console is awkward because the headlamp flasher button is tricky to find.

The electric starting is so reliable now that it seems hardly worth a mention. Neat, though, is the easy control of warm up idling speed by the cold start lever, particularly as the GS750 is a bit cold blooded.

The tool kit is small but effective and all the routine servicing is simple to perform. The air filters are washable foam and a check on oil level can be made through the sight glass on the clutch cover.

Like Kawasaki, Suzuki have made the best of the chain final drive without enclosing it. Each link of the massive ¾-in pitch chain is sealed with O-rings and its adjustment at roughly 600 mile intervals, even in wet weather, was the only attention the bike needed.

In performance, handling and comfort, the Suzuki is almost top of its class first time out. Attention to the brakes could well make it perfect.

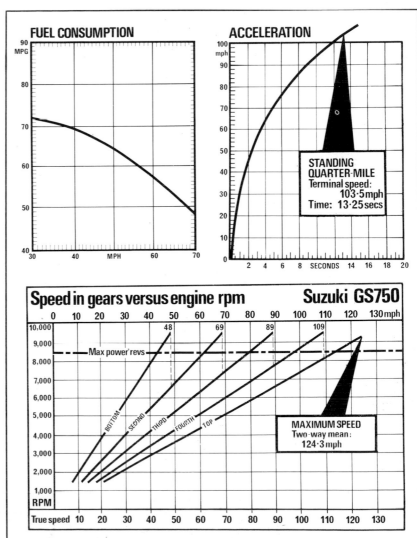

FUEL CONSUMPTION

ACCELERATION

STANDING QUARTER-MILE
Terminal speed: 103·5mph
Time: 13·25 secs

Speed in gears versus engine rpm — Suzuki GS750

Max power revs

MAXIMUM SPEED
Two-way mean: 124·3 mph

Triumph Trident T160

Few modern roadsters have a racing record as enviable as the Triumph Tridents and BSA Rocket Threes. American veteran Dick Mann used a BSA 750 cc three to win the Daytona 200 classic in 1970, John Cooper had some memorable wins at Mallory Park and Ontario, California, on a 750 cc Triumph and a production version took four wins on the trot in the Isle of Man Production TT.

However, it can be argued that the legend that these wins created lead to the downfall of the triples, for after development for racing by the fabled Doug Hele, the machines were very reliable, while the production versions were anything but that. It seemed that the factory were content to rest on their winner's laurels . . .

A result of the way it was derived from the 500 cc twin Triumph, the Trident was notoriously complex and costly to manufacture despite it only having pushrod valve operation. It was bugged by the old problems of oil leaks from the engine and front fork, even on the final T160.

This was the best triple made. It was fast, with a top speed of 120 to 125 mph and impeccable handling, while it boasted such up-to-date features as electric starting, full instrumentation and a low and sleek profile.

It was undoubtedly one of the best looking Tridents made. In the classic Triumph mould it had a beautiful teardrop shape tank, swept back handlebars, a low seat and a pair of upswept silencers that set off the lines of the machine perfectly. Had it not been for the crippling cost of its manufacture and the unfortunate collapse of the Norton-Villiers-Triumph empire, the Tridents would still be rolling out of Small Heath. As it is, manufacture stopped in late 1976.

The last Trident, the T160, boasted all the features found on the earlier T150. The engine was a three-cylinder, set across the frame with the two camshafts in the crankcases and pushrods to the valves. A 120-degree spacing between the crank throws gave the machine its distinctive exhaust note. Primary drive to the dry, single plate clutch was by a triplex chain. The gearbox was the same five speed version found on the 650 and 750 twins. An electric starter drove the engine through a ring gear on the clutch.

Major difference of the T160 was that the cylinders were canted forward in the interests of weight distribution, as on the BSA Rocket Three which went out of production in 1972.

The T160 was lower, sleeker and longer than the old T150 model and much more comfortable to ride. The changes to the bike started at the front forks which were lowered by using shorter springs. The mudguard had a plate mounting at the slider instead of the previous fragile tubular brackets.

The new instrument cluster with its warning lamps was bolted to the new top yoke.

The frame, derived from Les Williams' four-times Production TT-winner 'Slippery Sam' racer, was shallower overall but still allowed the engine to sit 1 in higher than before for better ground clearance and a lower seat height.

Specification

Engine: 740 cc (67 × 70 mm) overhead valve, transverse, in-line three. Light-alloy cylinder block and head. Four main bearings; two plain, one roller timing side, one ball drive side; plain big ends. Dry sump lubrication. Compression ratio, 9·5 to 1. Three 27-mm Amal carburettors with lever-operated air slides; paper-element air filter. Claimed maximum power, 58 bhp at 7,250 rpm.

Transmission: Duplex 0·437 in pitch primary chain with slipper tensioner. Dry single-plate clutch and five-speed gearbox. Overall ratios: 12·72, 9·04, 6·89, 5·85 and 4·92 to 1. Final drive by 0·625 × 0·375-in chain. Mph at 1,000 rpm, 15·5.

Electrical Equipment: Coil ignition with ballast resistor. 12-volt, 15-amp-hour battery and 120-watt alternator with zener-diode charge control. 7-in diameter headlamp with 45/40-watt main bulb. Starter motor, direction indicators.

Brakes: Hydraulically-operated 10-in diameter disc front and rear.

Tyres: Dunlop TT100, 4·10 × 19-in front and rear.

Suspension: Telescopic front fork. Pivoted rear fork with three-position spring preload adjustment.

Frame: Duplex tube cradle with forged lugs.

Dimensions: Wheelbase, 59 in; seat height, 30·5 in; ground clearance, 6·5 in; overall length, 88 in, turning circle, 19 ft 6 in; all unladen.

Weight: 518 lb including one gallon of fuel.

Fuel Capacity: 4·8 UK gal (5·8 US gal).

Oil Tank Capacity: 6 pt.

Manufacturer: Norton Villiers Triumph Ltd, North Way, Walworth Industrial Estate, Andover, Hants.

Performance

Maximum Speeds (Mean): 119·5 mph; 100 mph with rider in two-piece outfit sitting normally.

Best One-way Speed: 124·8 mph — dry track, slight tail wind.

Braking Distance — from 30 mph: 27 ft 3 in.

Fuel Consumption: 37·6 miles/UK gal (31·2 miles/US gal) overall.

Oil Consumption: 238 mpp.

Minimum Non-snatch Speed: 13 mph in top gear.

Speedo Accuracy:

Indicated mph	30	40	50	60	70	80	90	100
Actual mph	29·4	39·8	50·1	59·9	69·8	80·5	90·9	101

The rear fork lengthened by an inch, brought the wheelbase up to 59 in.

The Trident T160 really shows its mettle when you stretch its legs on long, fast and bumpy bends. Despite rear spring rates that are on the soft side for good handling, the confidence and ease with which the T160 could be rushed along without drama was marvellous.

Wet weather handling is even better. On the worst greasy roads the London suburbs could offer, the Trident had fewer vices than most bikes have in the dry. There is a natural stability to the machine that is almost uncanny.

The suspension and frame are not wholly perfect though. The rear fork has been weakened in its lengthening and this showed when it twisted after hitting bumps with two-up. The front fork suffered hydraulic lock on sharp bumps and clonked loudly. There were also leaks from the slider seals, although this was to be corrected by a better design.

Performance has changed little since the introduction of the original 1968 models. Although a three-into-two collector exhaust system had been adopted to spread the mid-range torque and cut noise levels, the three-cylinder engine produces most of its torque in the top end of the rev range. It burbles along nicely and controllably at low revs but gives its best above 4,500. It seemed to make hardly any difference whether you changed up at 7,000 or 8,000 rpm – the Trident surged along with just the same urgency.

Gearing is slightly lower than the original Tridents, but the latest model easily equalled the earlier ones on top-end speed. With a two-way mean of 119·5 mph and a best of almost 125 mph it makes the Trident one of the fastest machines in 1976.

In practice, however, the lack of low end torque did not reflect this potential. Sitting up in a two-piece outfit, the best the triple could achieve was a mean 100 mph in top gear. This was mainly because of the large gap between fourth and top was not matched to the power characteristics. With the gearbox a compromise derived from the twins it did not allow a fine adjustment of the gear ratios for optimum results. Nevertheless, the Trident is perfectly capable of sustaining an easy 90 mph two-up on the open road.

Engine vibration was not quite down to the levels of most four-cylinder machines, but at the same time was never worrying. There was a resonant patch around 4,500 rpm that is transmitted mainly through the footrests. Handlebars are rubber-mounted – the footrests should have been, too.

The gearchange is noiseless and slick, losing nothing in the change to the left side. Most changes on the move were clutchless but the dry clutch managed to lose its fine adjustment and slipped during the acceleration tests. Had the clutch been up to scratch, 0·2 seconds would have been cut from the quarter-mile time of 13·8 sec.

For general use the proportions of seat and handlebars are superb. With a height of only 30½ in the seat is low enough for all but the shortest to stand astride. It was long and well padded, too, with plenty of room for a passenger.

For fast riding however, the footrests are still too far forward, even though they have been moved back by 1 in on the left and 2 in on the right compared to the T150. The result is that, at any speed over 60 mph, too much weight is placed on the arms. The factory's answer is that they could not move the pegs back any farther because the kickstart lever is in the way.

The tank is a work of art. Beautifully styled, it holds over 4½ gallons, useful as the Trident averaged a very poor 37·6 mpg in everyday use, giving a range of just over 170 miles. But when using even five-star fuel, some pinking was experienced at small throttle openings.

Oil consumption was similarly poor at 238 mpp, although much of this may have been due to the leaks from the primary chaincase and the rev-counter drive. The chaincase leak, from the clutch cable entry point, is caused by the drilling breaking into the inner casing. Owners can cure it by pressing a steel tube through into the clutch operating casing.

Starting from cold is reliable provided the rider floods each carburettor (the middle one by means of the lever, the others with the tickler buttons) and closes the air slides. Touching the button brings a resounding clunk as the staring

gear engages and the engines fires up.

The new thumb switches for the left hand are also a vast improvement on the old Lucas items but they suffered from internal corrosion of the contacts.

The Trident's braking is absolutely stunning. Once bedded in, both the front and rear Lockheed discs were capable of sensitive howling stops at the limit of the Dunlop TT100 tyres' adhesion.

Hydraulics on the rear unit are much better than the Commando 850 Mark III, being tucked away behind the silencer mounts with the master cylinder filler under the seat.

Lighting, although only from a conventional 45/40-watt headlamp, is good enough for 60 mph riding at night. The dipped beam projected a strong fan-shaped beam with good cut-off.

Like all Triumphs, the Trident had a remarkably accurate speedo – within 1 mph correct up to 100 mph.

Typically British, the Trident demonstrates the skill of the development men to make the best of what is basically a crude modification of a smaller twin-cylinder machine. Had the management called for a design that started from scratch, Britain might have still had a strong industry.

A British classic, The Triumph Trident in its final T160 form was a thrilling machine to ride with fine handling and good top end power. Poor detail design spoilt it and industrial disasters killed it off

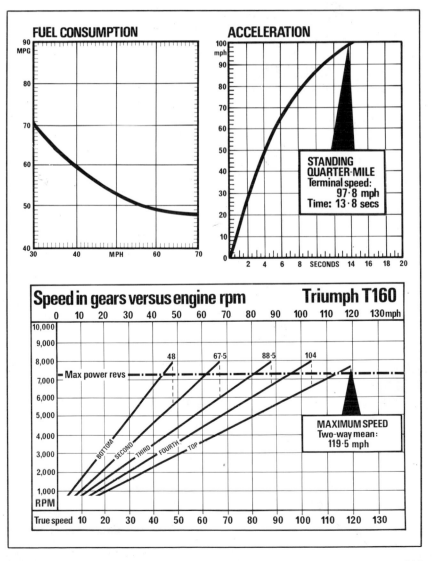

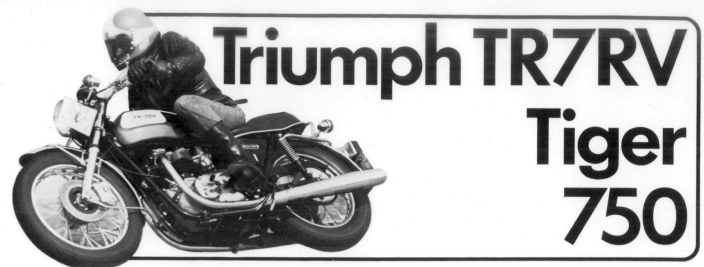

Triumph TR7RV Tiger 750

A lot of industrial history has been made since the then-new 744 cc Triumph Tiger was tested back in February of 1973. At that time it was being built at Meriden under the BSA-Triumph group banner: but that banner was already in tatters, and later in the year came the shotgun marriage with Norton Villiers.

Rightly or wrongly, the new management declared Meriden would be closed and sold, that Triumph twins were 'outdated' and would be dropped in favour of the more modern Nortons.

The outcome was the famous sit-in, and the ultimate formation of a workers' co-operative to purchase and re-open the Meriden factory. The Bonneville 750 came back into production and, now, Prince Charming has also kissed its single-carburettor cousin, the TR7RV Tiger 750.

Substantially (and understandably), the model is as it was when put to sleep in 1973, with the only major changes a hydraulically-operated disc brake instead of drum-type and, of course, the transfer of the gear pedal to the left side as required by transatlantic regulations. There are, too, later-pattern silencers, and a new and

attractive fuel-tank colour scheme of deep bottle-green and ivory.

Rather oddly, in the interim, the overall weight (as checked on the MIRA weighbridge) appears to have crept up by around 30 lb, and not even the makers can suggest a reason. Even so, at 448 lb the Tiger is still just about the lightest seven-fifty around, which is why it can give a very noble account of itself, notwithstanding the fact that its power output of 49 bhp at 6,200 rpm is out-gunned by more exotic rivals.

It is unsophisticated – but relaxing with it. At 70 mph, the machine is merely ambling along, the motor turning over lazily on little more than a smidgeon of throttle. This gait can be kept up for mile after mile, hour after hour, with the minimum of effort by rider or engine.

During the time the bike was in our hands, it came in for a variety of uses, including motorway dashes, a trip to the Victory Trial in mid-Wales, a two-up tour, and general town and country utility work. From all of this it emerged with a 46 mpg fuel consumption – rather disappointing, and some 12 mpg down on the corresponding 1973 model.

No logical explanation could be found, but possibly the pads of the disc brakes at front and rear rub the surface lightly when in the 'off' position and contribute to this increase in consumption.

The use of front and rear disc brakes can be regarded as an advance when applied to racing bikes – but they seem hardly necessary on this type of roadster, for they perform no better than

Triumph fan Bob Currie, Midland Editor of Motor Cycle, *takes the Tiger 750 for a spin near its home, the Meriden factory near Nuneaton in Warwickshire*

Following pages: Sports version of the TR7RV Tiger 750 – the Bonneville 750

117

good twin-leading-shoe drum brakes. The TR7RV's stopping figure from 30 mph was a quite commendable 30 ft 4 in. However, the same model stopped in 30 ft when fitted with a rear drum brake.

On the road, a two-finger stroke of the lever was enough to cut the speed, and at the same time the disc gave a slightly more positive feel to the rear brake pedal. But it is all a matter of what one gets used to, and there will still be a strong body of unconvinced sceptics.

So how did the discs perform in rain? There

though, slick and positive.

One thing the Tiger can provide is a big helping of power from way low down, and that shows up in the acceleration figures; around 14 sec for a standing quarter-mile from a 'cooking' seven-fifty cannot be bad!

For the standing quarter-mile, we gave it the whole dragster treatment – lean-forward stance, smoky, snaking getaway. Wheelies, even. However, we were not impressed with the almost knobbly tread of the standard K70 rear tyre and reckon we could have got better figures with the

Specification
Engine: 744 cc (76 × 82 mm) overhead valve, parallel twin. Light-alloy cylinder head; cast-iron block. Roller drive-side, ball timing-side main bearings; plain big ends. Dry sump lubrication; piston pump. Compression ratio, 7·9 to 1. Amal 30-mm choke carburettor with lever-operated cold-start slide. Claimed maximum power, 46 bhp at 6,200 rpm. Maximum torque, 42 lb-ft at 5,300 rpm.
Transmission: Triplex 0·375-in pitch primary chain. Wet, multiplate clutch and five-speed gearbox. Overall ratios: 12·25, 8·63, 6·58, 5·59 and 4·7 to 1. Final drive by 0·625 × 0·375-in chain. Mph at 1,000 rpm in top gear, 16·1.
Electrical Equipment: Coil ignition. 12-volt, 10-amp-hour battery with charging by alternator, rectifier and zener diode. 7-in diameter headlamp with 45/40-watt main bulb.
Brakes: Hydraulically-operated 10-in diameter disc front and rear.
Tyres: Dunlop Gold Seal K70, 3·25 × 19-in front, 4·00 × 18-in rear.
Suspension: Telescopic front fork. Pivoted rear fork with three-position spring preload adjustment and Girling dampers.
Frame: Duplex tube cradle with 2·5-in diameter spine.
Dimensions: Wheelbase, 57·5 in; seat height, 32 in; ground clearance, 7·5 in; handlebar width, 26 in; castor angle, 62°; trail, 4·5 in; all unladen.
Weight: 448 lb, including one gallon of fuel.
Fuel Capacity: 4 UK gal (4·8 US gal) including 4 pt reserve.
Oil Tank Capacity: 4 pt.
Manufacturer: Meriden Motorcycles Ltd, Meriden Works, Allesley, Coventry, Warwicks.

Performance
Maximum Speeds (Mean): 112·4 mph; 96·6 mph with rider in two-piece suit sitting normally.
Best One-way Speed: 116·3 mph – dry track, slight three-quarter tail wind.
Braking Distance – from 30 mph: 30 ft 4 in.
Fuel Consumption: 46 miles/UK gal (38·2 miles/US gal).
Oil Consumption: negligible.
Minimum Non-snatch Speed: 18 mph in top gear.
Speedo Accuracy:

Indicated mph	30	40	50	60	70	80	90
Actual mph	29·6	39·9	50·1	59·9	69·6	79·3	89

was very little rain during the period of the test, but on the one-and-only rain-showery day (and it would be the one we picked to do the touring story!) they caused no worry.

The Triumph is really comfortable. The seat height of 32 inches might seem a little high, but is compensated for by giving the seat a narrow nose, so the rider can reach the ground without strain. However, the seat could do with being a couple of inches longer. If the rear face of the seat were to be vertical, instead of sloping forward at top, it would make all the difference when carrying a passenger.

Ideally, a footrest position about an inch or two more to the rear would have been better but this, of course, is dictated by the position of the gear pedal. The pedal is slightly too far in front of the rest, and upward changes were best made by moving the foot forward until the heel was pivoting on the footrest; it came as second nature after a while. It is an excellent gearchange,

K70 HS version fitted to the previous TR7RV or a TT100.

The use of a K70 studded tyre on the front was difficult to understand, too, and with 1,800 miles on the speedometer, the tread showed distinct signs of ratcheting.

However, that did not seem to affect the handling, and the extent to which the model could be laid over in complete confidence was evidenced by the flat ground away on the centre-stand extension pedal.

At low speed, the steering was rather heavy on first acquaintance, growing lighter as speed rose, but the novelty of this soon wore off and, thereafter, it was accepted as normal.

There is some vibration present, at some sectors of the range, but it would not be a true-born Triumph if there were not. We have to confess that the Tiger was a whole lot smoother at 70 mph than some Triumphs we have ridden.

On the other hand, after putting it full-whack

through the timing traps for a 113 mph mean you realise there are more sophisticated models around. Take it above the 6,000 rpm mark, and you get the distinct impression that there is a lot of machinery clanking around.

All right, so there may be. But on most highways, the number of chances of whacking a bike up to 113 mph can be counted on the fingers on a boxing glove. In more conventional riding conditions, the Tiger 750 does very well.

This is one of ye olde-fashioned machines which does not have the nicety, or the complex-

ities, of an electric starter. The very long-shanked kick starter is more than adequate to spin the crankshaft over with little muscular effort.

For once, here was a Triumph which did not call for the morning ritual of freeing the clutch plates, and although it did appreciate closing of the air lever for the first few seconds, that could be opened again almost immediately.

The air lever is mounted, somewhat inconveniently, on the front face of the air cleaner box and it had the annoying habit of partly closing itself with the machine in use. Something else the factory might consider relocating is the re-setting knob of the trip odometer drum. This is shrouded by the headlamp shell, and proved nigh-on impossible to operate without the expenditure of a large number of cuss-words.

On the credit side, there was nary a drip of oil on the garage floor in nearly three weeks of use; and the centre stand was one of the best we have come across, requiring just a flick of the toe to hoist the model at almost the centre-point of balance, making access to either wheel a simple matter.

Another good point was the speedometer – when checked against MIRA's electronic timing gear it proved to be spot-on accurate, all the way up to the top of the scale. So, ninety on the clock really was ninety, with nothing added for rider flattery.

A fast, night-time run through the twisty lanes of the upper Teme Valley showed the effectiveness of the 45-watt main headlamp filament and, on switching to the motorway, a 70 mph after-dark cruising speed was held with ease.

The green 'main beam' indicator lamp in the top face of the headlamp shell was too bright and distracting, which sorely tempts you to cover up this new-fangled nonsense with a strip of sticking plaster.

And that, really, is about all that there is to say. The TR7RV Tiger 750 is a Triumph in the traditional style – lively, gutsy, tractable, and with the handling bred of a whole basket-full of production race victories.

If, performance-wise, it works out at just about on a par with the Bonnie, then that's the Bonnie's hard luck. Why have two carbs, when you can do it all with one?

Rear wheel of the Triumph Tiger is no longer the fabled quick release unit but a built-up hub with a disc brake

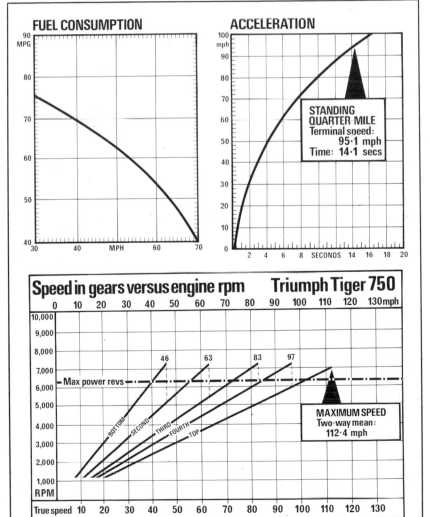

Yamaha XS750

In these days of increasing conformity in motor cycle designs from Japan, Yamaha's double overhead camshaft XS750 triple is something of a rarity – a bike of distinctive character and class with an extremely competitive price tag. Furthermore, it is a mature motor cycle. Yamaha could have very easily been drawn into the speed race that gripped the 750 cc roadster class in 1977. Instead, the XS750 is uniquely appealing for its flexibility, riding comfort and highly sophisticated equipment.

Should its specification, which includes a tough shaft drive, cast-alloy wheels and three disc brakes, two on the front, one on the rear, sound like the perfect touring bike, then that is just a bonus in the deal. The XS750 can still give a good account of itself. Top speed approaches 120 mph and it can easily cruise at over 100 mph.

With that sort of performance it does not make the bike sensitive to constant maintenance. The shaft drive precludes chain tensioning and a typical neat touch is the use of rubber boots over the control levers to keep out water. However, the engine unit itself is enough to stand out in a crowd. Displacing 747 cc with an almost square bore and stroke of 68 by 68·6 mm and with the

two overhead cams chain driven from the left-hand end of the crankshaft it has its three throws set at 120 degrees like the now defunct Triumph Trident. The exhaust gives off the same rorty, warbling note from the two silencers.

Only a light pull is needed to open up the three 34-mm choke constant-velocity carburettors and the engine immediately sets to the task. The power band is broad and full and although it peaks out at a maximum of 64 bhp at 7,500 rpm there is never any real need to approach this for fast riding. There is more than enough urge up to 5,000 rpm and, better still, with plenty of flywheel inertia on the crankshaft you do not get any of the annoying lurching between gear changes so familiar on the bigger fours.

Inevitably, with the more direct drive between the crankshaft and rear wheel resulting from a Morse-type primary chain to the clutch and a set of spur and bevel gears to the shaft from the five-speed gearbox, the gear change is a lot less crisp than on other, chain-drive Yamahas. But it is still better, particularly in the lower ratios, than the BMW gearbox with its mainshaft running at higher speed.

Despite the 7,500 rpm rev-counter red line, the Yamaha spins smoothly to 8,000 rpm through the gears for maximum acceleration. But with an all-up weight of 553 lb with the 3¾-gallon tank full, it is hardly surprising that the flat out acceleration is less potent than most seven fifties. The standing quarter-mile time of 14·1 sec is about seven tenths down on the best in the class but on a par with the 750 cc BMW. Even so, the

Rapidly becoming a classic in enthusiast motor cycling circles, the Yamaha XS750 has a double overhead camshaft three-cylinder engine and shaft drive, plus an uncommonly mature approach to design features that riders really need

Specification

Engine: 747 cc (68 × 68.6 mm) double overhead camshaft transverse, in-line three. Four plain main bearings; plain big ends. Wet sump lubrication with trochoid pump and replaceable oil filter. Compression ratio, 8.5 to 1. Three 34-mm choke Mikuni CV carburettors with lever-operated cold-start jets; oil-soaked foam air filter. Claimed maximum power, 64 bhp at 7,200 rpm. Maximum torque, 46 lb-ft at 6,000 rpm.

Transmission: Primary drive by inverted-tooth Morse Hy-vo chain. Wet, multiplate clutch and five-speed gearbox. Overall ratios: 13.29, 8.64, 7.07, 5.96 and 5.2 to 1. Final drive by spur and bevel gears and cardan shaft. Mph at 1,000 rpm in top gear, 14.5.

Electrical Equipment: Coil ignition. 12-volt, 14-amp-hour battery and 225-watt alternator. 7-in diameter with 45/50-watt sealed beam unit. Starter motor; four fuses; self-cancelling indicators.

Brakes: Hydraulically-operated 10.4-in diameter double-disc front, single-disc rear.

Tyres: Bridgestone, 3.25H19 ribbed front, 4.00H18 patterned rear studded; Avon Roadrunners, 4.10H19 front, 4.25/85H18 rear on test machine. Yamaha cast-alloy seven spoke wheels.

Suspension: Kayaba telescopic front fork. Pivoted rear fork with five-position spring preload adjustment.

Frame: Duplex tube cradle-type with pressed-steel gusseting.

Dimensions: Wheelbase, 58.75 in; seat height, 33 in; ground clearance, 7 in; handlebar width, 27 in; trail, 4.5 in; castor angle, 63°; turning circle, 15 ft 6 in; all unladen.

Weight: 531 lb including one gallon of fuel.

Fuel Capacity: 3.75 UK gal (4.5 US gal). Vacuum-controlled taps.

Sump Oil Capacity: 6.5 pt.

Manufacturer: Yamaha Motor Co Ltd, 2500 Shingai, Shizuoka-ken, Tokyo.

Performance

Maximum Speeds (Mean): 117.1 mph; 104.2 mph with rider sitting normally.

Best One-way Speed: 122.3 mph – dry track, three-quarter tail wind.

Braking Distance – from 30 mph: 28 ft 3 in.

Fuel Consumption: 40.9 miles/UK gal (33.9 miles/US gal) overall.

Oil Consumption: Negligible.

Minimum Non-snatch Speed: 14 mph in top gear.

Speedo Accuracy:

Indicated mph	30	50	70	90
Actual mph	31.0	49.8	69.9	90.4

zero to 60 mph time of 6 sec gives the rider plenty to play with on the road. And with plenty of low end power the pick up from low speeds is more deceptive than the more highly tuned models.

The weight of the Yamaha may have produced its apparent thirst for fuel. The overall figure we returned was 41 mpg during the test but this included a large proportion of motorway travelling. More typical may be the 50 mpg we obtained in one cross country run and the average 45 mpg obtained from a bike equipped with a full fairing in a 5,000 mile run across North America.

As a touring machine, there are few bikes to better the XS750, even among higher-priced models.

Riding comfort is excellent despite the high-frequency buzz that the engine emits above 5,000 rpm. The dual seat is deeply padded and the rubber-mounted handlebar is given just the right amount of sweep at the grips for a balanced lean into the wind at over 70 mph. The depth of the seat padding makes it very high at 33 in and this might be awkward for shorter riders trying to balance the bike when stationary. But the height of the seat lessens the possibility of cramping the legs on a long run and gives a similar layout to the BMW.

The test machine, which had 3,000 miles clocked when collected, was fitted with Avon Roadrunner tyres in 4.10H19 and 4.25/85H18 sizes as replacements for the standard Bridge-stones. The British covers suited the bike admirably.

Steering is neutral and precise and the bike never needed anything more than a nod from the

Setting a new fashion in superbike design is the shaft drive and supple suspension of the Yamaha three

rider to whistle steadily through fast corners.

Suspension, in keeping with the touring image, is soft and remarkably compliant at speeds below 50 mph where it is in fact better than a BMW. The front fork sliders have stick-free Teflon bushes that prevent the transmission of small bumps and ripples. A measure of their effectiveness is that even running across a series of lane marking studs on the motorway, the ride was never anything less than perfectly smooth.

The price you pay for such superlative riding comfort is indifferent high speed handling in bends. The rear suspension has slack damping that produced a slow pitching in corners above 80 mph, and lighter riders reported a slight weave in a straight line above speeds of 100 mph.

An advantage of the Avon front tyre was that its slightly larger diameter made the speedometer spot-on accurate to 100 mph.

Braking is provided by three $10\frac{1}{4}$-in diameter stainless-steel discs with floating calipers. As on previous Yamahas, the front double disc brake needs a hard pull on the hand lever, but the rider is rewarded with progressive power.

The rear wheel also suffered from hopping if the brake pedal was stamped on imprudently when pulling up from high speed. The 28 ft 3 in stopping distance from 30 mph is more a reflection of the grippiness of the tyres than the power of the brakes.

Apart from the 50/40-watt sealed beam Stanley headlamp, which with its broad spread is only average in power, the electrics are otherwise excellent.

Lamps and instruments are big and bright and the self-cancelling indicators are a positive safety advantage. Firing up on the electric starter never failed. The petrol taps are operated by the vacuum from the outer two inlet tracts.

Not content with building one of the better all-round motor cycles on the road, Yamaha have gone a stage further and eased maintenance tasks.

An eighteen-piece toolkit includes Allen keys for all the engine covers and there is even a loop of cable to compress the rear suspension to aid rear wheel removal.

One additional convenience is that the rear half of the rear mudguard hinges up to aid wheel removal – but why are other factories not capable of offering it?

The Yamaha XS750 leaves the rider with the pleasing impression that he has been thought of when the bike was conceived; that the test riders covered a lot of miles when putting it through its paces and that the designers expected the bike to be more than just a flash in the pan.

How right they are; the bike is already very popular with the touring rider and for 1978 should satisfy those who want more power too. Camshafts with higher lift and more overlap plus a capacitor-discharge ignition that further reduces the Yamaha's limited maintenance, gives a performance more in line with the other Japanese seven fifties.

Even now, the XS750 looks set to be a classic.

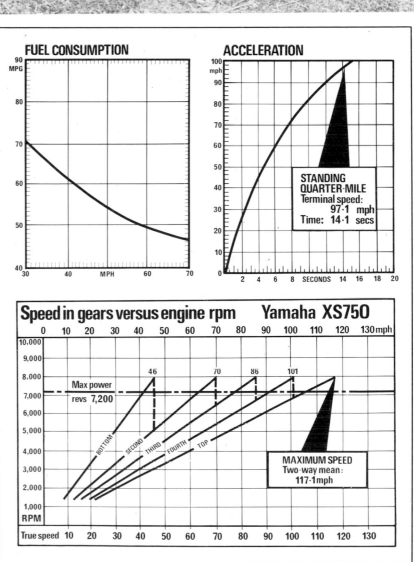

FUEL CONSUMPTION

ACCELERATION

STANDING QUARTER-MILE
Terminal speed: 97·1 mph
Time: 14·1 secs

Speed in gears versus engine rpm   Yamaha XS750

Max power revs 7,200

BOTTOM   SECOND   THIRD   FOURTH   TOP

46   70   86   101

MAXIMUM SPEED
Two-way mean: 117·1mph